10-MINUTE
MINDFULNESS

71 Simple Habits for
Living in the Present Moment

S.J. SCOTT & BARRIE DAVENPORT

ISBN-13: 978-1546768289

ISBN-10: 1546768289

Disclaimer

Contents

Your Free Gift

As a way of saying thanks for your purchase, we're offering a free companion website that's exclusive to readers of *10-Minute Mindfulness*.

With the companion website, you'll discover a collection of printable mindfulness checklists, affirmation worksheets, and bonus videos. See the link below to get free instant access.

MindfulnessHabit.com/10mm

Hyperlinks Included in This Book

The digital version of *10 Minute Mindfulness* includes over a hundred hyperlinks to resources and tools that can help you self-educate. But if I included them here, it would have resulted in a clunky paperback reading experience (and also a frustrating one because some websites will change or delete their links in the future).

That's why I've compiled all the websites mentioned in this book on my blog: **www.developgoodhabits.com/10mmnotes**

If you'd like to learn more about a specific tool or resource mentioned, then I recommend checking out this page and bookmarking it for future reference.

Again that's **www.developgoodhabits.com/10mmnotes**

Happy reading!

PART I

INTRODUCTION

You drag yourself out of bed after slapping the snooze button for a third time, already twenty minutes behind schedule.

As you check the clock, your brain pumps out a quick shot of oh-crap-I'm-late adrenaline, and you hit the ground running.

The TV blares in the background with another day of bad news and political discord, tainting the morning with despair before you make it to the shower.

As your brain tries to process the morning news, you remember all you have going on today: A few meetings. A project due. A doctor's appointment. Carpool duty for the kids.

And, oh yeah … the clash you had with your boss yesterday. Your mind loops through the conversation a few times, and you feel angry all over again.

You step out of the shower to hear your phone dinging with emails and texts. Your heart rate speeds up, and low-level anxiety buzzes through your body like a double-espresso aftershock.

Showered, dressed, and already agitated, you make your way to the kitchen to grab a quick breakfast to go, while your kids bicker over the last doughnut and your spouse is freaking out about lost car keys.

By the time you make it to work, or to the carpool line, or wherever you go to begin your day, your mind is frazzled and distracted. Your inner world roils like the first tremors before a volcanic eruption.

When you're so pumped full of adrenaline and anxiety, your body and mind become addicted to the drama, negativity, and distractions of daily life. This addiction keeps you stuck in a pattern of knee-jerk reactions to thoughts and events, rather than allowing you to consciously create what you want from the day.

By evening, you're too burned out to enjoy family time, hobbies, or relaxation. Instead, you crave something mind-numbing, like a few hours of TV or surfing the net, before you fall into bed.

Can you identify with this scenario?

It may not exactly describe your daily life or morning routine, but you've likely experienced some version of it before. Distraction. Stress. Worry. Agitation. Negative thinking. Emotional exhaustion. *Physical* exhaustion. All of these play a much bigger role in our lives than we care to admit.

More often than not, our days don't begin peacefully and joyfully. In fact, we feel far from calm, centered, and present, and it takes a toll on our happiness and mental health.

The Trap of Unconscious Living

This scenario we just described comes from a vicious cycle of reactivity, distraction, and stress that can be best described as "unconscious living."

Most of us are unconscious of the ways our lifestyle choices, habits, and thoughts create unhappiness and anxiety.

We are unconscious of our true values, life priorities, and our deeper longings for a more balanced way of life.

We are also unconscious of the vast peace and contentment available in the present moment because we are so preoccupied with past regrets and worries about the future.

Says British philosopher, writer, and speaker Alan Watts:

> We are living in a culture entirely hypnotized by the illusion of time, in which the so-called present moment is felt as nothing but an infinitesimal hairline between an all-powerfully causative past and an absorbingly important future. We have no present. Our consciousness is almost completely preoccupied with memory and expectation. We do not realize that there never was, is, nor will be any other experience than present experience. We are therefore out of touch with reality. We confuse the world as talked about, described, and measured with the world which actually is. We are sick with a fascination for the useful tools of names and numbers, of symbols, signs, conceptions and ideas.

If you see yourself as unconscious and out of touch with reality (and most of us are), there's nothing "wrong" with you. Unconsciousness isn't a character flaw or mental defect. It isn't something you were born with.

In fact, you may have noticed that small children don't suffer from unconsciousness. They are thoroughly and completely engaged in the present moment, whether it's good or bad.

They delight in the simplicity of a flower. They can fall asleep on the floor when they are tired or scream like a banshee in public when something upsets them. For a child, there are few filters between the moment and the response.

Unconsciousness is a learned behavior we develop over time. But it's also a byproduct of the way our brains react to perceived threats and how we respond to the societal, cultural, and technological input we receive (in massive volumes) every day.

As we discussed in our book, Declutter Your Mind, "The human nervous system has been evolving for 600 million years, but it still responds the same as our early human ancestors who faced life-threatening situations many times a day and simply needed to survive."

As a result, we are wired for a "negativity bias"—a tendency to react to negative stimuli more intensely than positive experiences. This is true *even* when we don't face the same life-threatening scenarios. Our life-threatening situations come in the form of rumination, regret, and worry.

Modern technology has poured fuel on the flames of our anxieties. With access to 24/7 news, advertising, and information, we're exposed to a profusion of "phantom boogeymen" to fret about.

Am I attractive enough?

Smart enough?

Wealthy enough?

Happy enough?

Are my children safe?

Will the economy tank?

Am I eating the right diet?

Will I be washed to sea in a tsunami?

Will I be kidnapped by aliens?

Every day, every hour for many of us, we are bombarded with information that keeps us stirred up, worried, and chasing paper tigers.

There's no time to enjoy the moment because we're too busy preparing for the unforeseen future or replaying the pains of the past.

Our cellphones, laptops, and tablets have become weapons of mass distraction, pulling us further and further from the only place of real peace and happiness—the present moment.

Says Vietnamese Buddhist monk and peace activist Thích Nhất Hạnh in his book Peace is Every Step, "Life can be found only in the present moment. The past is gone, the future is not yet here, and if we do not go back to ourselves in the present moment, we cannot be in touch with life."

Easy for a Buddhist monk to say, right?

But many people discredit the idea of living in the present. They view it as unrealistic or a waste of time—something unattainable for everyday people who live in the modern world.

How can it be done? How can you remain in the present when you have to plan, schedule, achieve goals, and simply live life in a hectic world that's so focused on the future? Unless you're a monk or a hermit, is it possible to truly live in the now?

The answer is found through the daily practice of mindfulness.

The practice of mindfulness anchors you in the present moment, even if it's for just a few minutes at a time, and actually the best way to build this habit is to start with a few minutes at a time.

We're not suggesting you must be mindful all day, every day. We are inviting you to the *practice* of mindfulness, a habit you develop slowly and embrace as part of the way you want to live.

Is it even possible to be present for every single moment of your life?

No.

But you can use mindfulness practices to be *more present*.

For every minute you practice mindfulness in your day, you generate a reservoir of inner peace that can support you through the times of "unconscious living."

The more you practice mindfulness, the more present moments you'll savor and the *less unconscious* you will become. More of your actions and decisions will be grounded in awareness, allowing you to be responsive rather than reactive. Over time, you'll get into the habit of returning to the present when you find yourself trapped in the cycle of reacting to the demands of modern living.

What Is Mindfulness?

Mindfulness is very simple. **It means you become *intentionally aware* of the present moment while paying close attention to your feelings, thoughts, and sensations of the body.**

You pay attention on purpose and consciously direct your awareness to whatever you are doing or thinking. Washing dishes. Talking to your spouse. Playing with your kids. Working on a project. Doing nothing.

But mindfulness involves one further step—the practice of non-judgment.

Non-judgment is the key to experiencing the deeper benefits of a daily mindfulness practice. It requires that you observe your actions, thoughts, and feelings from a distance, without labeling them as good or bad, right or wrong.

Says meditation teacher and mindfulness author James Baraz in his book Awakening Joy, "Mindfulness is simply being aware of what is happening right now without wishing it were different; enjoying the pleasant without holding on when it changes (which it will); being with the unpleasant without fearing it will always be this way (which it won't)."

This detached awareness frees you from the stress associated with longing, regret, desire, and worry.

When you are truly *experiencing* the moment, rather than analyzing it or getting lost in negative thoughts, you enjoy a wide array of physical, emotional, and psychological benefits that are truly life changing. (More on these benefits later.)

The practice of mindfulness isn't rocket science. The difficulty lies in our ability to incorporate mindfulness into our daily lives. We have to learn *the habit* of mindfulness and create strategies for incorporating this practice into our daily lives.

Most of the people who read this book will have families, careers, responsibilities, and goals. Your life is probably very active and busy. This means you *already* have developed a number of routines that will be in direct conflict with the mindfulness practice.

As Buddhist meditation teacher Sharon Salzburg reminds us, "Mindfulness isn't difficult. We just need to remember to do it."

That's what we want to help you do with the habits outlined in this book.

The Purpose of 10-Minute Mindfulness

We want to give you practical tools to develop a mindfulness habit so you remember to do it often enough that it becomes automatic.

And we want to show you how to incorporate mindfulness into your entire day—from waking up to bedtime—so you easily return to present-moment awareness, even as you go through the normal activities of your day.

Mindfulness can be applied to anything you do. It doesn't require that you sit in the lotus position and meditate for hours. You don't have to wear strange clothes, take up yoga (unless you want to), or lock yourself away in a cave.

You don't need to belong to any particular religion to practice mindfulness, although mindfulness can be applied to your religious practice if you wish.

As we mentioned, practicing mindfulness simply means directing your awareness to what you are doing—whether it's completing a project at work or cleaning out the refrigerator.

However, we've taken the liberty of suggesting seventy-one daily mindfulness habits that you can accomplish in about ten minutes to make your practice of mindfulness more engaging, satisfying, and fulfilling without overwhelming you.

The habits outlined here either:

1. Provide an opportunity for mindfulness as you perform the habit;
2. Support a more mindful lifestyle with a behavior or mind shift;
3. Do both of these things.

Many of these mindfulness habits have been extensively researched and proven to provide a myriad of psychological and physical benefits, as we discuss later in the book.

Both Steve and Barrie practice many of these habits themselves and have experienced the benefits firsthand.

Says Barrie in her book *Peace of Mindfulness*:

> Through my own mindfulness practices, I have experienced every one of these benefits personally. I have used mindfulness to cope with and reduce anxiety, worry, and depression. During post-operative recuperation, I've used it to manage pain and the frustration of recovery time. I regularly practice mindfulness when going to sleep and notice I fall asleep much more quickly. When I practice mindfulness techniques in my daily life, I feel more content, calm, and emotionally balanced. I'm happier in my relationships and view the world and my experiences with a more positive perspective when I take the time to meditate or use other present moment techniques.

Steve is relatively new to the practice of mindfulness. It took getting married and seeing the birth of his son to teach him the importance of valuing the present moment over being a slave to his daily checklist. While he still enjoys working hard, he now proactively schedules time in his day to appreciate the small things in life.

Both Barrie and Steve make mindfulness an important part of their daily routine. And what they've found is that it doesn't take that long to build these small but important habits. In fact, you can do each of them in ten minutes or less.

Why Ten Minutes?

The key to developing any new habit (as you'll learn in Part II) is to start small and focus on consistency (instead of hitting a certain metric or milestone).

Unlike many other habits (like exercise, for example), the practice of mindfulness doesn't require that you spend hours of time on the activity. You can certainly work up to an hour-long meditation practice or create a long tea preparation ritual if you wish.

But most mindfulness activities require you to tune into the present moment for just a few minutes, making these habits some of the easiest you will ever undertake. Again, the key is remembering to do them throughout the day. (Fortunately, we have a number of suggestions for sticking to these habits that we'll cover in the next section.)

Although these mindfulness habits are easy to practice and don't take much time, there are a large number of benefits from this daily practice. So, let's move on to discuss the benefits of mindfulness and how to build these habits into your day.

Links and Resources

One last thing before we dive into the content: you'll quickly notice that this book is chock-full of links to many books, resources, and websites. They're included here because each can help you take that next step to build a specific habit.

While we provide a detailed overview of each habit, you might want to learn more about the practice and how to fully incorporate it into your life. So with each habit, we've included at least one additional resource you can check out if you'd like to take your self-educational efforts to the next level.

Finally, you don't have to write down resources mentioned in this book **because all of them are also included on the companion website.**

Well, now that you know what to expect from this book, let's get started by talking about the benefits of mindfulness and the process for building this type of habit.

PART II

BUILDING MINDFULNESS
HABITS

10 Benefits of Building Mindfulness Habits

For those who are frequently pulled away by the usual preoccupations of daily living (and isn't that most of us?), mindfulness affords a richer appreciation of the moment and a larger perspective on life. It also helps us alter our habitual responses by pausing long enough to choose how we act.

These benefits of mindfulness fall into three categories:

1. They improve your physical and mental well-being;
2. They reduce or slow down some symptoms of physical illness;
3. They minimize the frequency and intensity of destructive or negative emotions.

To clarify these three points, here are ten benefits of how mindfulness can have a positive physical and emotional impact on your life.

#1. Mindfulness reduces rumination and overthinking.

Rumination is a maladaptive form of self-reflection that has an addictive quality. When you're constantly "in your head," looping negative thoughts, brooding, and thinking about the past, you put yourself at a much greater risk for mental health problems like depression and anxiety.

Research studies support that practicing mindfulness helps reduce rumination. In a study by Chambers et al. (2008), participants (with no previous meditation experience) in a mindfulness meditation retreat reported significantly higher mindfulness, less rumination, and fewer symptoms of depression than the control group.

#2. Mindfulness alleviates some stress.

A mindfulness practice can decrease the levels of the stress hormone cortisol, according to the results of the Chambers et al. study (as well as numerous other studies). The study shows a direct connection between resting cortisol and scores on a mindfulness scale.

#3. Mindfulness improves memory, concentration, and performance.

Mindfulness practices have been shown to improve focus, memory, and reading comprehension, as well as reducing mind-wandering. Students who practice mindfulness show they perform better on tests than those who don't.

Researchers at Massachusetts General Hospital revealed in a study that regular meditation causes the brain's cerebral cortex to thicken. The cerebral cortex is responsible for higher brain functions like memory, concentration, and learning.

#4. Mindfulness helps with emotional reactivity.

Daily stressors in our lives impact our ability to maintain emotional stability so we don't react with anger and emotional outbursts. Mindfulness helps us respond to stressful situations in calmer, healthier ways.

A study by Ortner et al. (2007) showed that mindfulness meditation allowed participants to disengage from emotionally upsetting pictures and focus better on a cognitive task, as compared with people who saw the pictures but did not practice mindfulness meditation.

#5. Mindfulness promotes cognitive flexibility.

Cognitive flexibility is the ability to change your train of thought quickly to adapt to the demands of the situation. A 2009 study revealed that the practice of mindfulness meditation promotes cognitive flexibility and helps our thinking to be less rigid and more creative.

#6. Mindfulness creates happier relationships.

A University of North Carolina study of "relatively happy, non-distressed couples" found that the couples who actively practiced mindfulness saw improvements to their relationship happiness. They experienced less stress in their relationships and were able to cope with challenges more easily.

#7. Mindfulness reduces anxiety.

Mindfulness practices help shrink the amygdala—the fear center of the brain. The practices increase the prefrontal cortex to promote a calmer, steadier brain. The practice of detachment and non-judgment of anxious thoughts and feelings helps lessen fearful reactivity to the thoughts.

#8. Mindfulness improves sleep.

Insomnia and sleep problems are common stress reactions. Mindfulness habits promote calm and reduce rumination that can disrupt sleep.

A 2015 study of older adults confirms that mindfulness meditation practices support getting a better night's sleep. According to the study, mindfulness meditation can "increase the relaxation response through its function of increasing attentional factors that impart control over the autonomic nervous system."

#9. Mindfulness promotes mental health.

University of Oregon researchers found that a mindfulness technique called "integrative body-mind training" can result in brain changes that may be protective against mental illness. The practice of the technique "induces positive structural changes in brain connectivity by boosting efficiency in a part of the brain that helps a person regulate behavior," according to the study.

#10. Mindfulness provides pain relief.

A variety of studies support the findings that mindfulness practices help people with chronic pain to relieve symptoms and cope with pain. Mindfulness helps people notice pain without judgment, as negative thoughts and judgments exacerbate pain. These practices also afford a more accurate perception of pain, reducing the secondary suffering that comes with evaluating and worrying about pain. Researchers have seen a reduction in pain intensity and a lessening of pain unpleasantness with participants who practiced mindfulness meditation.

With repetition of these habits, an intentionally created state of mindfulness can become an enduring trait as a result of the long-term changes in brain function and structure.

Just as an exercise habit will change your body, a mindfulness habit will literally reshape your mind.

Now, let's discuss the fundamentals of creating new habits so that mindfulness can become an automatic practice you apply throughout your day using some of the habits outlined here.

How to Develop a Mindfulness Habit

Many of the mindfulness habits outlined here will be new to you, and you'll have to learn how to incorporate a brand new activity into your day.

However, some mindfulness habits are different from building new habits. Becoming more present doesn't always mean you'll form a habit from scratch. Instead, it often involves replacing an existing habit with a better version of the same habit.

In many ways, this is similar to replacing a bad habit with a good one. The routine is *already* there. All you need to do is swap out an existing routine with an improved (more mindful) version.

Let me give a concrete example of this. Every day Joe makes and drinks a cup of tea at 8 a.m. He drinks it because he enjoys the taste and needs a jolt of caffeine to get his motor running before the day begins.

With Joe's tea-drinking habit, he does everything on autopilot. He makes the tea as part of his multitasking process in his preparations to leave for work. He slurps down his tea while driving to work. Sometimes he does these actions so efficiently that he's unsure if he even had his morning cup of tea.

In contrast, with a mindfulness version of the tea-drinking habit, the main thing Joe will need is time. He will need time to make the tea without other distractions. And he will need time to mindfully enjoy the cup of tea. The routine is in place; he just needs to account for the extra time the improved mindful version will take.

So let's dive into the nine-step process for building mindfulness habits.

Step #1: Decide on the changes you want to make.

The first step of turning these ideas into action is to make a list of all the habits you'd like to build. (Hopefully our list of seventy-one mindful habits in this book will spark a few ideas.) Sit down with a pad of paper and a pen (or your favorite note-taking app) and make a detailed list of the habits you want to add or change.

It's important that these changes are what *you* desire. It's easy to get fired up by the idea of being more mindful, but it does take some concerted effort. Becoming more mindful may sound great, but you may need to make some sacrifices to create the changes you want in life.

Step #2: Inventory existing habits.

With your list of behaviors to change in hand, sit down and study your daily routine. How many of these habits would you like to do in a more mindful manner?

We all have specific habits that we do every day. Hopefully, you don't need to create a "habit" to talk to your spouse. But you will need to make sure the communication with your spouse is conducted in a more mindful manner.

As you go through your list of existing routines, think about your desired mindful habits. Note the overlap between the two groups. When you find habits that potentially overlap, these should be the first habit changes you tackle.

Since these habits already exist, they are easier to change. All you need to do is make the conscious decision to go about these habits in a more mindful way.

Step #3: Limit the number of habits you try to change.

In the book Willpower, authors Roy F. Baumeister and John Tierney described a concept known as *ego depletion*, which is a person's "diminished capacity to regulate their thoughts, feelings, and actions."

Simply put, our willpower is like a muscle. It weakens throughout the day because of constant use.

Baumeister and his colleagues have tested ego depletion in a variety of scenarios. One was called the radish experiment. They brought three groups of people into a room and offered a selection of food (before the participants worked on a puzzle): pieces of chocolate, warm cookies, and radishes.

> » One group could eat anything they wanted.
> » Another group could only eat the radishes.
> » The final group wasn't given any food options.

After that, each group was moved into a separate room, where they had to work on a challenging puzzle. The groups that didn't previously exert willpower (i.e., they ate whatever they wanted or weren't given a food option) worked on the puzzle for an *average of twenty minutes*. The group that had to exert willpower and resist the tasty treats worked on the puzzle for an *average of eight minutes*.

What does the experiment show?

It's simple: most people can resist temptations, but this effort leaves us in a "weakened" condition where it becomes harder to tap into that pool of willpower. People don't achieve peak results with a task because of motivation. Instead, the number of decisions and completed tasks ultimately determine their level of success with a new task.

This leads to two important lessons that will ultimately determine your success at forming habits:

» You have a finite amount of willpower that becomes depleted as you use it.
» You use the same stock of willpower for all manner of tasks.

It's important to recognize that your levels of willpower (and therefore motivation) will decrease as the day goes on. This means that if you'd like to make any significant, lasting change in your life, you need to focus only on building a handful of habits at once— preferably as part of a single routine, which we'll talk about later.

Step #4: Commit to a minimum of 30 days for your new habits.

Mindfulness will improve the quality of your life and your connection with others. But creating these good feelings doesn't mean the process will be simple or painless. In fact, it's best to not expect an overnight change. In fact, it will probably take you a few weeks to retrain your mind to think differently.

Some people say it takes twenty-one days to build a habit, while others claim it takes up to sixty-six days. The truth is that the length of time varies from person to person and from habit to habit. You'll find that some habits are easy to build while others require more effort. So, our advice is to commit to a few mindfulness habits for the next thirty days *at a minimum.*

During this time, your entire life should be structured around carving out daily time to practice your new mindfulness habits.

Step #5: Anchor your mindfulness habits to an established routine.

A mindfulness habit *shouldn't* be based upon motivation, fads, or temporary desire. Rather, it should be instilled into your life to the point where the behavior becomes automatic. This often means you don't need a sophisticated series of steps—just something you can commit to. Day in and day out … without fail.

A great example of this comes from B.J. Fogg and his "Tiny Habits" concept. What you want to do is to commit to a very small habit change and take baby steps as you build on it. An important aspect of his teaching is to "anchor" the new habit to something you *already* do on a daily basis.

> » *"After I make my first cup of coffee in the morning, I will mediate for ten minutes."*
>
> » *"After I arrive at the office, I will sit down and identify the three important tasks that I'd like to accomplish for the day."*

> » *"Before dinner, I will shut down all electronic devices and encourage my family to do the same thing."*

You get the idea. Find a habit you do consistently, and anchor your new behavior to it.

Step #6: Take baby steps with your new habits.

The key to habit developing is to make micro-commitments and focus on small wins.

Mindfulness takes a while to become habitual. Major mindfulness habits (like mindful eating and mindful conversations) will overturn a lifetime of experience. It isn't easy. Don't be ashamed if at first you only act mindfully part of the time. Instead, learn to celebrate the fact that you were able to make a bit of progress.

You need to revel in successes and simply remind yourself to work at it better the rest of the time. Mindfulness change is often measured by baby steps, but it gets easier the more you do it.

If you have problems keeping up with your mindful habits, try making micro-commitments.

A micro-commitment is a goal so small it seems impossible to fail. With these commitments, it's more important to stay consistent and not miss a day than to hit a specific milestone. What you'll find is that when you have a low level of commitment, you'll be more likely to get started.

Here is an example of a mindful habit micro-commitment. Rather than committing full-on to mindful eating, commit to doing it for the first dozen bites of every meal. A commitment this small should not impact your lifestyle in any way. But that is what makes it powerful.

First, it builds the routine of using the mindful habit every single day *without fail.*

Second, when you start doing something mindfully, you will often continue to do so. You make the "commitment" for a dozen bites, but in three out of four meals, you may find yourself eating mindfully for the entire meal. Because being mindful is, in fact, more enjoyable.

Step #7: Make a plan for potential obstacles.

All new habits have obstacles, even mindful habits. While many mindful habits are variations of an existing habit, you may still face resistance to these new patterns.

For instance, you might occasionally think:

"Eating mindfully adds ten minutes to my meal. I don't have that much free time today."

Or:

"I am too angry to have a mindful discussion; I want to vent my rage."

The items above are two common obstacles people may encounter using mindfulness on existing habits. Typical obstacles include:

  » Time
  » Pain
  » Weather

» Space

» Costs

» Self-consciousness

The key is to understand that these obstacles happen to everyone, and you can plan for them. That way, when they occur, you won't feel blindsided by these negative experiences.

The simplest way to manage potential obstacles is create "if-then statements" for what you'll do when certain challenges arise.

Here are a few examples:

» *"If I check the weather and it's raining, then I will work out at the gym instead."*

» *"If I don't have time for my project at the end of the day, I will start to wake up thirty minutes earlier and work on it before anything else."*

» *"If I have a bad day and don't feel like expending my energy on mindful communication with my spouse, I will give him/her five to ten mindful minutes of my time then explain my bad day and feelings."*

» *"If I am running short of time at mealtime, I will commit to taking my first three bites in a mindful manner."*

By having a plan for those occasional challenges, you can overcome pretty much any obstacle that comes your way. My rule of thumb is to come up with a series of if-then statements for *all* the common challenges that occur in life.

Step #8: Reward yourself for reaching important milestones.

Building new habits doesn't have to be boring. Actually, you can turn it into a fun process by building a reward system into the process. The reward you pick is up to you, but it shouldn't be something that runs counter to the intent of the goal. For instance, if you have a goal of mindful eating, don't reward yourself with a gluttonous visit to an all-you-can-eat buffet.

The reward doesn't need to break the bank. You could check out a new movie, enjoy a night out with your significant other, or simply do something you love. (And if you get stuck, then check out the article in the companion site on 155 ways to reward yourself.)

Step #9: Introduce more mindful habits.

Becoming more present in life may take dozens of habits, which might seem like a lot of new behaviors. But one of the great things about mindful thinking is that it spreads like a virus. The more areas of your life in which you are intentional, the more this mindfulness will spread to other parts of your thinking.

Put simply: the more you practice mindfulness, the more natural it becomes.

Due to this fact, we recommend that you review the following list of seventy-one habits every few months because you'll probably discover many small actions that you initially dismissed that have now become more relevant to your personal situation.

The good news is that by this point, "mindfulness" should be almost second nature. The major obstacle at this point will be simply adding new habits to your routine. Keep repeating as needed until you feel you are completely mindful in your life, mind-set, and actions.

Now that you know *how* to create a mindfulness habit, let's dive into the seventy-one changes that can be incorporated into your busy day.

How to Use These 10-Minute Mindfulness Habits

We've organized these seventy-one mindfulness practices into habits that can be completed in the morning, afternoon, or evening, with many ideas for each part of the day.

Again: We are not suggesting that you attempt to develop all these habits.

Instead, we recommend a "choose your own adventure" approach where you review the list to determine which mindfulness practices appeal to you the most.

Start by adding a couple of the following mindfulness habits to your day. You might choose to do one in the morning first because this is when you have the most energy and focus, which will make creating your new habit easier. However, you might find some mindfulness practices for the afternoon or evening that appeal to you more, so it's fine to choose one of these times.

Some of the habits are very easy to develop (like mindfully drinking a glass of water in the morning). Other habits, like meditation or journaling, will require more time and focus in order to incorporate into your daily schedule.

If you are new to developing habits, or you've had difficulty in the past sticking to your habits, start with a simple mindfulness practice first. These easier habits can serve as triggers for more difficult habits later on. For example, smiling in the mirror in the morning might trigger you to begin writing in your journal.

Also, consider your personal goals related to developing a mindfulness practice to help you decide which habits to choose first. Ask yourself:

» Would you like to find relief from anxiety or depression?

» Are you trying to reduce worry, stress, and overwhelm?

» Do you want to improve your focus and productivity?

» Would you like to become more centered, calm, and emotionally balanced?

» Are you dealing with an illness or want to improve your physical well-being?

» Do you want to improve the intimacy and quality of a relationship?

» Are you hoping to simplify your life?

» Do you want more self-awareness with a better understanding of your desires and motivations?

Knowing your personal goals can help you decide where to focus your efforts in developing mindfulness habits.

Finally, with each habit, we'll talk about the benefits of adopting it, the specific action steps **required** to build it, and links for additional information if you want to learn more about the concept.

Now let's dive into the seventy-one mindfulness habits for each part of your day.

PART III

··

MORNING MINDFULNESS HABITS

#1. Wake up Early

We began this book with a narrative that's all too familiar. We roll out of bed in the morning at the last minute, groggy, irritated, and already behind schedule. With little time to spare, the day begins like a headlong race against the clock, run in a haze of distraction and mindlessness.

We don't give ourselves the time in the morning to prepare for the day ahead. We don't allow time for thoughtful reflection, for connection with our loved ones, or just to begin the day slowly and peacefully. Sometimes we don't even have time to eat breakfast.

When you wake up late, everything is rushed and harried, and this sets the tone for the rest of the day.

Even ten extra minutes in the morning can give you time to plan your day, practice a short morning meditation, or write a gratitude list.

Choosing to awaken a little earlier in the morning not only allows you to begin your day with mindfulness but also extends the amount of time you have to enjoy life.

Says eighteenth century English educator and writer Philip Doddridge, "The difference between rising at five and seven o'clock in the morning, for forty years, supposing a man to go to bed at the same hour at night, is nearly equivalent to the addition of ten years to a man's life."

Imagine what you can do with ten extra years.

We won't lie to you—becoming an earlier riser isn't the easiest habit to establish. It's challenging to force yourself out of your warm and cozy bed when you don't have a compelling reason to do so. But if you wake up just ten minutes earlier, you'll be able to slow down the pace of your morning and adopt one of the other mindfulness habits we've included here. Those ten extra minutes can have a powerful effect on your state of mind.

If your immediate reaction is, "I don't want to wake up earlier. I need all the sleep I can get," we invite you to shift your thinking and give it a try for a week or so. You may be surprised at how much more you enjoy your mornings with just a few extra minutes.

Over time, you may discover that the early morning is your best time of day, a time that sets you up for success and joy throughout your day.

Action Plan: The best way to change your wake-up time is to do it gradually. Start with ten minutes earlier for a week or so until you (and your body) become accustomed to it.

If you normally get up at 7:00 a.m., don't suddenly change it to 5:00 a.m. Try 6:50 a.m. first to help you develop the early waking habit. Sudden changes to your wake-up time of an hour earlier or more are difficult to sustain. You'll have a sleep deficit that will discourage you from continuing this habit.

Slowly back up your wake-up time by five to ten minutes a week until you eventually reach your desired time. You might set a future goal of waking thirty minutes to an hour earlier. Much more than that may have a negative impact on your sleep, which is so essential to your mental and physical health.

You may need to adjust your bedtime as you work your way up to an earlier wake-up time. Check out mindfulness habit #70 for an evening wind-down ritual that can help you prepare for a good night's sleep.

If you find you have trouble getting out of bed, there are many strategies you can use to overcome this challenge:

» Put your alarm clock across the room so you are forced to get up to turn it off.

» Use an app called "Step Out of Bed" (it costs $1.99 for an iPhone), which won't shut off until you get out of bed and take thirty steps.

» Try the Alarmy app (free for Android users), which will not shut off until you get out of bed and take a picture of a pre-selected item in your home.

» Focus on timing your rest according to your sleep cycle. It has been reported that the average sleep cycle is ninety minutes, which is repeated throughout the night. If your sleep patterns match these cycles, then you'll wake up feeling refreshed and energized. Using an app like Sleep Cycle will help you make sure that you're getting a full night's rest.

» Avoid using a snooze button, which gives you mental permission to fall back asleep. This can make it even harder to get up and get moving.

» Adopt Nike's "just do it" attitude about getting out of bed. Don't let the sleepy voice in your head have any power. Just get up and start your morning routine.

» If you tend to fall back into bed after getting up, a great solution is to make your bed the minute you step out of it. You could even place a stack of books or other items on top of the bed to discourage you from climbing back in.

» Consider getting a coffee maker with a timer so you can hear and smell the coffee being made at your designated wake-up time.

Finally, the best strategy is to give yourself an inspiring reason to get up earlier. If having more time in the morning doesn't do it for you, find something that does. Maybe it's planning a walk with a friend or having a sit-down breakfast with your family. Maybe it's just taking a few minutes to drink your coffee while staring out the window and *feeling* grateful. Having something you look forward to can be a great impetus to throw the covers back and start your day.

Learn More: We recognize that it's not easy to rise early when you still feel groggy from the night before. So if you follow the suggestions we outlined and still have trouble getting out of bed, then I'd recommend the *"Snooze-Proof" 5-Step Wake-Up Strategy*, written by Hal Elrod, author of *The Miracle Morning* book series.

#2. Awaken with Gratitude

What better way to begin your morning than with a practice of gratitude? Adopting this mindfulness habit can shift your morning thoughts from those based in dread, anxiety, or apathy to more positive and contented thoughts.

In his book *The Art of Forgiveness, Lovingkindness, and Peace*, Buddhist practitioner and teacher Jack Kornfield says this about the practice of gratitude:

Buddhist monks begin each day with a chant of gratitude for the blessings of their life. Native American elders begin each ceremony with grateful prayers to mother earth and father sky, to the four directions, to the animal, plant, and mineral brothers and sisters who share our earth and support our life. In Tibet, the monks and nuns even offer prayers of gratitude for the suffering they have been given.

Gratitude is a mindfulness habit that awakens us to the large and small blessings we experience every day—those we tend to overlook in the busyness of our hectic lives. When we begin the day with gratitude, we train our minds to look for the positive rather than focusing on the challenges, frustrations, and slights we have encountered throughout the week.

The practice of gratitude not only grounds us in the moment when we reflect on our blessings. It also improves our health and well-being. The world's leading scientific expert on gratitude, Robert A. Emmons, PhD, has conducted multiple studies on the link between gratitude and well-being and confirms that practicing gratitude increases happiness and reduces depression.

Gratitude can improve your relationships, your self-esteem, and even your sleep according to these studies.

The key to making this habit effective is not the number of things you feel grateful for or even the amount of time you spend in gratitude, but rather the intensity of focus and feeling you have around the effort. A mindful gratitude practice means immersing yourself in the emotion so that you feel deeply and profoundly blessed.

Action Plan: Use your morning alarm as a trigger to begin your ten-minute gratitude habit. We suggest you keep a gratitude journal and pen next to your bed so you don't even have to move to begin the practice first thing in the morning. (Obviously, don't do this if you're also looking to combine this with the "wake up earlier" habit.)

Keeping a gratitude journal is a great way to reinforce your feelings of gratitude and to keep a permanent reminder you can refer back to often. Rather than writing a laundry list of gratitude items every day, we recommend choosing one or two gratitude items to focus on each morning for several minutes.

This allows you to fully reflect and meditate on each blessing so you can experience more profound and lasting feelings of gratefulness, as well as remain attentive and focused as you reflect.

Here is a four-step process to implement this habit idea:

1. Write down a gratitude item in your journal using words like "I am grateful for my warm and comfortable bed."

2. Pay attention to how you feel in your bed, and notice how warm and comfortable it is.

3. Direct your thoughts to some of the specifics of your comfortable bed—the soft sheets, the fluffy pillow, the mattress that keeps you off the floor and supports your body, the way the bed allows you to have a good night's sleep.

4. Think about what life would be like without this thing you are grateful for, like the bed in our example here.

5. You might think, "Without this bed, I would have to sleep on the floor or the couch. I would be cold and uncomfortable and wouldn't sleep well." These observations enhance your feelings of gratitude.

Follow similar steps for each gratitude item you write down. Direct your attention to the details of what you feel grateful for. If there are physical or emotional feelings involved, focus your thoughts on these feelings. Then consider how life would be without this thing you are grateful for.

Learn More: If you'd like to delve deeper into a mindful practice of gratitude, read this article, "How to Practice Gratitude Even When You Don't Feel Like It," and check out this gratitude course.

Also, **Barrie has created a gratitude worksheet that you can access on the free companion website**.

#3. Do a Mindful Body Scan

A fundamental application of mindfulness is getting in touch with how your body feels first thing in the morning. Your body can reveal so much about your mental and emotional state if you pay attention to what it is telling you. And the simplest way to get in touch with how you're feeling is to do a mindful body scan.

A body scan is a meditative practice in which you focus on each part of every area, often beginning at the toes and moving to the head. The key here is to train your attention on each specific part for a moment and pay close attention to how you feel.

By noticing each part of your body and the tension stored in different muscle groups, you can consciously release the tension and become more self-aware of what's behind the tension as you quiet your mind. Any discomfort or pain you may feel can be latent emotions you are storing that need to be acknowledged and released.

Performing a body scan also helps shift your attention away from your thoughts so that you become more grounded in your own physical presence. Just as breathing is a way to bring you back into the present moment, a body scan anchors you to the present as well.

Action Plan: You can do a body scan while you are still in bed before getting up. Lie flat on your back, and take a few deep and cleansing breaths. Allow your breathing to slow down, and try to breathe from your abdomen instead of from your chest.

Starting with your toes, direct your attention to each part of your body, slowly moving up from your toes, to your feet, ankles, calves, knees, thighs, etc., until you reach your face and head. If you wish, you can include internal organs as well, like your heart or lungs.

As you place your attention on each part of your body, notice any pain, tension, or tightness you're feeling. Do you notice a feeling of concentrated "energy" around a certain area? Focus for a minute and notice what you're feeling.

If you feel tension, discomfort, or pain in a part of your body, ask yourself, "What is the source of this feeling? What do I need to address or release?"

You may or may not get a clear answer to this, but pay attention to anything that comes to mind as you ask. So much tension and pain come from negative thoughts and emotions.

After asking these questions, take a deep breath and release the breath into the painful body part to relax this area. Visualize the muscles relaxing and the pain dissipating.

Follow the breath with a slow stretch if that works for the body part (e.g., you can stretch your facial muscles but not your head). Stretch your toes and the muscles in your feet. Move your feet in a circular motion to stretch your ankles. Flex your feet to stretch your calves. Breathe into each stretch for further relaxation.

After you complete the body scan, take a few more deep breaths, allowing your entire body to relax into the floor or bed. Be careful not to fall asleep if you intend on getting up and starting your day.

Learn More: If you'd like to expand your body scan practice, check out this 25-minute guided body scan meditation.

For more information on stretching exercises, check out these six full-body stretches. You can practice the stretching exercises as a separate mindfulness practice without the body scan if you wish.

#4. Practice a Morning Breathing Exercise

Do you pay much attention to your breathing? Breathing happens so naturally that most of us don't notice it unless there's a problem. But breathing is essential to our physical and mental well-being, and it helps connect the body and the mind.

As Buddhist monk Thích Nhất Hạnh says, "Breath is the bridge which connects life to consciousness, which unites your body to your thoughts."

Breathing is physically important for two reasons: it supplies our bodies and organs with the oxygen necessary for survival, and it rids our bodies of waste products.

But breathing is also the foundation for any mindfulness practice, as it helps you anchor your attention and calm your body and mind as you inhale and exhale while watching each breath.

Practicing mindful, focused breathing, even for ten minutes a day, reduces stress and promotes relaxation. Slow, deep, rhythmic breathing causes a reflex stimulation of the parasympathetic nervous system, which results in a reduction in the heart rate and relaxation of the muscles. Also, oxygenation of the brain tends to normalize brain function, reducing anxiety and stress levels.

You can enhance the mental and physical benefits of breathing by practicing a few minutes of deep or complete breathing every day. The complete breath, which is practiced in yoga, involves the entire respiratory system and employs all of the muscles.

The complete breath is part of yogic breathing exercises called *pranayama* in Sanskrit, meaning "controlled breath." It is believed to help balance the body's life force energy (known as prana), which promotes physical, spiritual, and mental health.

Action Plan: Here's a simple process to practice the morning breathing exercise:

1. Sit on the side of your bed or in a chair with your back straight and your feet planted on the floor.
2. Inhale slowly until your lungs are filled to capacity. Breathe in through your nose and push your stomach forward gently, as though you are filling your stomach. This is called abdominal breathing.
3. At the end of the inhalation, pause for a count of two.
4. Exhale slowly, smoothly, and completely, and gently allow your

stomach to return to its normal position. Pause at the end of the exhalation as well.

5. When you first begin, don't take too full a breath at once. Start by breathing to the count of four, pausing for the count of two, and exhaling to the count of four.

6. Keep your attention focused on the process of inhaling to the count of four, holding the breath for the count of two, and then exhaling for the count of four. If your mind wanders, gently bring it back to your breathing.

7. Repeat the breathing cycle ten times or for ten minutes.

Learn More: If you'd like to learn more about mindful breathing and how to use it to reduce anxiety and stress, check out this video on deep breathing exercises.

You might also enjoy the book *The Yoga of Breath: A Step-by-Step Guide to Pranayama* by Richard Rosen.

#5. Notice Your Thoughts

It may seem as though your thoughts have incredible power over you, and in a way, they do. Your thoughts can trigger anxiety, unhappiness, and anger. They can keep your mind trapped in a cycle of longing and negativity.

This cycle happens because we are unconscious of our thoughts, and we allow them to run rampant in our brains without challenging them or attempting to rein them in. Rumination becomes a bad habit, almost an addiction, that can undermine the quality of our lives.

If you allow negative thoughts to run rampant first thing in the morning, you lose the best time for creativity and productivity. Many people wake up feeling anxious and filled with dread, as the cycle of rumination and negative thinking begins the minute their feet hit the floor.

Once you're aware of this bad habit, you can begin to change it by adopting a very simple new habit—observation. When you separate yourself from your thoughts and simply notice them with detachment, you remove some of the power they have over your emotions.

As bestselling author and spiritual teacher Eckhart Tolle says in his book The Power of Now:

> Don't judge or analyze what you observe. Watch the thought, feel the emotion, observe the reaction. Don't make a personal problem out of them. You will then feel something more powerful than any of those things that you observe: the still, observing presence itself behind the content of your mind, the silent watcher.

When you become the silent watcher of your thoughts, you detach from them and the emotional power they have over you. They no longer define you or control you. The longer you practice observing your thoughts, rather than identifying with them, the more contentment and inner peace you'll experience.

Action Plan: Sit in a quiet place where you won't be interrupted for ten minutes. If you have family in the house, you might tell them not to bother you during these few minutes.

Close your eyes and take five slow, deep diaphragmatic breaths (as described in the previous breathing exercise). Breathing helps ground you in the present and calm you enough to become the "silent watcher" of your thoughts.

Imagine yourself sitting in a chair inside of your brain, as the observer of your thoughts. This visualization helps you separate yourself from the thoughts you are observing.

Wait for a thought to enter your mind and simply notice it. You might even say to yourself, "There's a thought entering my brain."

If the thought triggers an emotion, like anxiety or sadness, notice the emotion without judging it. You might say to yourself, "That thought triggered the feeling of sadness." Don't linger on the emotion or judge yourself for having it. Just move on to observing the next thought.

Notice the patterns and frequency of your thoughts and how they arise spontaneously, even as you sit and observe. See them as powerless objects that float in and out of your mind, like blowing leaves or clouds.

As you come to the end of this ten-minute time, remind yourself that your thoughts are not you and they have no power over you. By observing them as "blowing leaves," you will reduce the emotional triggers they produce, giving you more peace of mind and contentment.

Take a few more cleansing breaths, open your eyes, and move on to the activities of your day.

Learn More: Watch this video of author and mindfulness pioneer

Jon Kabat-Zinn discussing why and how to observe your thoughts to disempower them.

#6. Make Your Bed Mindfully

Do you make your bed every morning? It may seem like a waste of time on a rushed morning, but there are many great reasons to adopt this simple habit.

Making your bed is considered a "keystone" habit. As Barrie says in her book *Sticky Habits*, "Keystone habits are particular habits that make success in many other aspects of life far easier, regardless of the circumstances you face. These habits unlock a cascade of positive behavior changes with far less effort than establishing a single habit from the ground up."

Many other successful people believe in the simple but important habit of making your bed. In a commencement speech at the University of Texas, US Navy Admiral William H. McCraven said the following to the graduating class:

> If you want to change the world, start off by making your bed. If you make your bed every morning, you will have accomplished the first task of the day. It will give you a small sense of pride, and it will encourage you to do another task, and another, and another. And by the end of the day that one task completed will have turned into many tasks completed.

Making your bed in the morning is correlated to more productivity, a sense of well-being, and even better budgeting skills. It sets the tone for accomplishment throughout your day when you complete this one task the moment you get out of bed.

Having a neat, tidy bed makes your room feel less cluttered and chaotic, even if you have other things lying about. The smooth blankets, the tucked-in sheets, and the plumped-up pillows give a sense of completion to a night of sleep and a fresh beginning to a new day.

Rather than rushing through this task as though it's a chore you need to push through, view bed-making as a mindfulness ritual that's enjoyable and satisfying. Seeing the results of your efforts makes you feel accomplished and proud first thing in the morning, even though bed-making is a mundane task.

Action Plan: Before you get out of the bed, spend a few moments feeling gratitude for your comfortable bed. Many people in the world don't have a comfortable, clean bed to sleep in, so acknowledge the blessing of this luxury.

Think about the warmth you feel under the covers, the softness of the blankets and sheets, and the comfort of your pillow. Consider how your bed supports you as you restore your body and mind during sleep.

When you get out of bed, first remove the pillows and set them aside. Then pull back the comforter, blankets, and top sheet.

Smooth out the wrinkles in the fitted sheet and pull each corner tighter under the mattress. Notice how neat and smooth the fitted sheet looks.

Then pull up the top sheet and smooth it out as well. Neatly tuck in the sides and bottom of the top sheet under the mattress. If you like, fold back the top edge of the sheet to create a crisp, hotel-like appearance. Take a moment to notice how neat your work looks.

Pull up the blankets and/or comforter so that it hangs evenly on each side of the bed. Smooth out all of the wrinkles, again noticing your work and appreciating how it looks.

You can complete pulling up your sheet and comforter while still in bed if you wish, getting out to pull everything up toward the headboard and place the pillows properly.

Plump your pillows and decorative pillows (if you use them), and place them on the bed as you like them. Smooth out any final wrinkles and tuck in any sheet edges that are showing.

Take a moment to enjoy the full effect of your neatly made bed. Mentally say, "Thank you," to your bed for supporting you through the night, and view your efforts at making it as an expression of gratitude for your bed.

Learn More: If you'd like to learn how to properly make your bed with fresh, clean sheets straight out of the wash using "hospital corners," check out this video demonstration.

#7. Follow a Bathroom Ritual

All of us have a morning bathroom routine we follow to get ready for the day. This routine is a series of habits that we conduct without much thought or attention.

You might get out of bed, use the toilet, wash your hands, brush your teeth, put in your contacts, strip off your clothes, hop in the shower, wash your body and hair, dry off, get dressed, apply makeup, fix your hair, and leave the room—all without thinking about any of the actions you're taking.

Going through this habitual routine mindlessly does streamline the process and may get you out the door more quickly. However, when your body is on autopilot, moving along without conscious direction, your mind is free to do what it wants—and often what it wants is to focus on stressful and negative thoughts.

Unfortunately, this mindless bathroom routine is a time when you are naturally prone to infect your day with these anxiety-producing thoughts. In fact, levels of stress hormone, cortisol, rise during the early morning hours and are highest about 7:00 a.m. You are already predisposed to anxiety in the morning due to this hormone surge, and your freewheeling thoughts are only adding to the problem.

Rather than allowing yourself to mindlessly march through this bathroom routine, view the steps you take to get ready in the morning as an attentive ritual rather than just a means to get out the door.

By paying more attention to the actions you take, you return to the present moment with focus and gratitude, rather than allowing your random thoughts to set the tone for the day.

Action Plan: You developed your morning bathroom habits years ago, maybe even when you were a child and your parents instructed you on proper self-care and hygiene. But there's a good reason "why" behind each of these habits.

Before you begin your habitual routine, take a moment to identify the reason behind your morning habits, and acknowledge each action with gratitude and appreciation.

Not to be gross here, but even using the toilet can be a mindful activity. Our bodies eliminate waste for a good reason. Most of us don't pay much attention to this bodily function (unless something is wrong), but it is a miraculous operation that keeps us healthy.

The excretory system helps to keep salts and urea from building up to dangerous levels and becoming toxic. Body waste prevents illness, cleanses our bodies from the inside out, and gets rid of excess matter that our bodies do not use.

We're not suggesting you create a lengthy "toilet meditation" but simply a moment of gratitude that your body is taking care of you by eliminating waste.

As you wash your hands, notice the lather of the soap and the warm water running over them and appreciate that your clean hands will keep you healthy.

When you floss and brush your teeth, remind yourself of how important and useful your teeth are—both for your health and your appearance. Clean them carefully with gratitude and pride.

As you shower and clean your body and hair, allow yourself to enjoy the warm water running over your body, the smells of the soap and shampoo, and the invigorating feeling you have once you complete your shower.

Proceed through each one of the actions in your bathroom routine by reminding yourself of why it is a necessary, positive, and useful part of your day. If your mind begins to wander and ruminate, gently direct your attention back to the task at hand.

If you notice a surge of anxiety or dread as you get ready in the morning, focus on your breath for a moment or two, and then return your attention to what you are doing. Don't attach to the feeling or recriminate yourself for having it. Acknowledge it, breathe, and move on.

Learn More: Watch this video of Jon Kabat-Zinn talking with Oprah Winfrey about his mindful morning routine.

#8. Practice Shower Meditation

For most people, a shower is already part of their morning routine. But when you add a quick meditation session to this ritual, you can focus on practicing deep thinking and creating positive thoughts for the day.

Sure, shower meditation might sound hokey, but look it this way: You know how you often get your best thoughts in the shower? Well, the same principle applies here. The calming effect of warm water puts your mind on autopilot, which frees it up to come up with inspirational ideas. (There's even research that shows we often get our best ideas while engaging in mindless tasks, like showering, driving, and doing chores.)

Action Plan: Shower meditation can easily be attached to your existing "getting ready" routine. This means you only need to add a few minutes to your shower time to get the full benefit of this habit.

Here's a five-step plan to practice show meditation:

1. Get started by letting the warm water of the shower wash over your body.

2. Visualize all the stress, anxiety, and worries in your life as being tangible things sticking to your skin.

3. Visualize the water and soap scrubbing the stress off your body.

4. Envision all the metaphysical "dirt" of your body—your fears, regrets, anxiety, anger, and stress washing free and swirling down the drain.

5. Realize that you are clean, fresh, and ready to start your day free of distractions.

Learn More: The website MindBodyGreen.com has a great variation on the shower meditation that takes only five minutes to complete.

#9. Drink Water

One of Barrie's most consistent morning habits is to drink a full glass of water as soon as she goes to the bathroom sink after awakening. She has done this for years and considers it essential to her morning routine. As the Slovakian proverb reminds, "Pure water is the world's first and foremost medicine."

There are so many health benefits to drinking a glass of water first thing in the morning. Your body has been without hydration for seven to eight hours, so it needs water to rehydrate—especially if you're going to follow up your water with a cup of caffeinated coffee or tea.

Drinking a large cool glass of water after you wake also fires up your metabolism by 24% for ninety minutes according to a research study. It also increases mental and physical performance during the day. When you're dehydrated, you can feel tired and drained, and you may experience headaches and mood fluctuations.

Drinking water on an empty stomach purifies the colon, which makes it easier for your body to absorb nutrients. Water plays an important role in weight loss, as it is essential for the removal of waste and metabolized fat from the body.

When you drink a full glass of water before breakfast, you feel full longer, helping you avoid overeating and mindless snacking.

The act of drinking water physically flushes out impurities, but it also symbolizes a clean, fresh beginning to a new day as you flush out the negativity, failures, and suffering you have stored inside of you.

You can create a mindfulness ritual by drinking a morning glass of water every day, especially when you affirm and focus on the symbolic and physical benefits of drinking water.

Says Buddhist monk and author Thích Nhất Hạnh, "When we drink a glass of water, and if we know that we are drinking a glass of water, if we're concentrated on the fact that we are drinking water, mindfulness is already there. And the water drinking becomes deeper, truer, and real."

Action Plan: We don't need to instruct you on how to drink a glass of water. You've been doing it for years, and it's fairly obvious. Fill glass, drink up.

Now, it might seem silly to regard drinking a glass of water as a mindfulness exercise, but slowing down our actions in even the most mundane habits can draw our attention toward the subtle things in life that might otherwise pass us by.

Drinking water is necessary for life, health, and emotional well-being, and we believe it's a habit worth savoring. A few simple shifts in your perspective and behavior can turn this simple act into a lovely ceremony.

Some people suggest filling a glass full of water before you go to sleep at night, covering it with a tissue, and keeping it on your beside table to drink upon awakening.

Barrie prefers to fill her glass with fresh, cool water while standing at the bathroom sink and looking in the mirror.

Steve, on the other hand, pours thirty-two ounces of ice-cold water with lemon into a Contigo water bottle. Why lemon? Because it promotes hydration, is a good source of vitamin C, and supports weight loss. Why the 32-ounce bottle of water? Because it helps him stay on top of his daily water intake. Drinking two of them throughout the day gives him the basic amount of water that people typically require.

As you fill your glass of water, feel gratitude for the easy access you have to fresh, potable water. In many developing countries, people must walk long distances for clean drinking water, or they must drink tainted water. Your fresh, safe water arrives instantaneously at the turn of a handle, with little effort from you.

Before you drink, look at the full glass of water and notice how inviting and clean it looks. Feel the coldness and wetness of the glass. Pay attention to how your mouth and body feel in anticipation of hydrating with water.

Look at yourself in the mirror (if one is in front of you) as you take your first sip. Watch yourself take the sip. Let the cool water sit in your mouth for a moment and run over your teeth, gums, and tongue. Then swallow it and visualize it refreshing and hydrating all of the organs and systems of your body.

Take more small sips, as well as some big gulps, noticing how you feel as you become more and more hydrated. Once you take the last sip, think about how the water in your body is now working on your behalf to keep you healthy and mentally sharp.

Learn More: If you want to further appreciate water and water drinking, read this article called "The Miracle of Water Mindfulness" to help change your relationship with water.

#10. Smile in the Mirror

After you've had your water, and if you are still standing in front of the mirror, this is an excellent time to practice smiling at yourself.

Does that seem ridiculous? It might feel that way when you first practice it (especially if someone walks in on you). But smiling at yourself in the mirror first thing in the morning has many positive benefits for your well-being. In fact, British research scientists concluded "that smiling can be as stimulating as receiving up to 16,000 Pounds Sterling in cash."

Smiling slows the heart and relaxes the body, and it releases endorphins that counteract and diminish stress hormones. It also has been shown to increase productivity while a person performs tasks.

According to several studies, smiling can trick your brain into feeling happy, even when you feel sad as you're smiling. Faking a smile or laugh works as well as the genuine article.

Your brain can't differentiate between a real or fake smile, as it interprets the arrangement of the facial muscles in the same way.

Smiling at yourself in the mirror can also boost your self-confidence, especially if you include some positive affirmations that you say out loud as you look at yourself smiling.

It only takes a few minutes to include a smiling habit into your morning routine, but the effects of your effort will extend throughout your day.

Action Plan: Yes, you will feel silly when you first begin this mindfulness practice. But enjoy the silliness and allow yourself to have fun with this new habit.

After a few weeks of practice, you'll notice how much you look forward to it and how it can get your day off to a more confident and lighthearted start.

Here's how to practice smiling in the mirror:

» Stand in front of your bathroom mirror and look at yourself.

» Notice how your face appears in repose. *Does it look neutral? Sad? Tense? Angry?* Just notice what you see without judging.

» Slowly allow a small smile to creep across your lips. Allow the smile to grow bigger until you can see your teeth. Don't worry if you feel the smile is fake—even if you feel unhappy or stressed. Just continue to smile at yourself, looking into your own eyes.

» If your cheeks or face begin to hurt, take a break and then go back to smiling. You might even get tickled and start to laugh, which makes your smiling habit more real and effective.

Give yourself a reminder to smile every time you see a mirror throughout the day to help keep your mood elevated.

Learn More: Read more about the science of smiling and why it is such a powerful gesture in this article.

#11. Practice Morning Meditation

Meditation is the centerpiece of a mindfulness practice. Taking time to meditate for just ten minutes a day will support all of your other daily mindfulness habits, as meditation is a form of strength training for your mind.

The purpose of meditation is to observe the patterns and habits of your mind and learn to tame the incessant chattering of your thoughts. With practice, you'll gain more and more control over your thoughts, rather than your thoughts controlling you and your emotions.

As Barrie states in her book *Peace of Mindfulness*, "The practice of meditation is a way to transform your mind by creating a beautiful state of stillness, silence, and clarity for sustained periods." The positive effects of meditation will saturate your entire day, making a morning meditation practice a perfect way to start your day.

There are dozens of physical and mental health benefits associated with a meditation practice. It:

» Lowers your blood pressure

» Boosts your immune function

» Decreases pain and inflammation

» Reduces anxiety and depression

» Improves focus and concentration

In addition, many religious traditions view meditation as a way to end suffering, enhance love and compassion, gain self-awareness, and ultimately reach a state of enlightenment.

Your goal for now is to simply develop the habit and strengthen your meditation skills.

Even a few minutes of meditation a day will provide the mental and physical benefits of the practice. In time and with practice, you'll notice that you are a more present, grounded, and content person.

Action Plan: If you wish, set a timer for ten minutes. Sit in a chair or cross-legged on the floor with a cushion. Keep your spine erect and your hands resting gently in your lap.

Close your eyes or keep them open with a downward focused gaze. Then take a few deep, cleansing breaths.

Become aware of your breathing. Notice the air moving in and out through your nostrils and the rise and fall of your chest and abdomen. Allow your breaths to come naturally without forcing them.

Begin counting your breaths, mentally saying the number as you exhale. Try counting backward from ten or, instead, think the word "in" as you inhale and "out" as you exhale.

When your thoughts wander (which they will do a lot in the beginning), gently return to the sensation of breathing. Don't judge yourself or your intrusive thoughts. Just lead your mind back to focused attention on breathing.

As you are breathing, you'll notice other perceptions and sensations like sounds, physical discomfort, emotions, etc. Simply notice these as they arise in your awareness, and then gently return to your breathing.

If you observe you've been lost in thought, view your thoughts as though you are an outside witness with no judgment or emotion. Label them by saying, "There are those intrusive thoughts again." Then return your attention to the breathing.

Continue with these steps until you are increasingly just a witness to all sounds, sensations, emotions, and thoughts as they arise and pass away.

As you end your meditation time, take a few more deep, cleansing breaths, open your eyes, and gently begin your day.

Learn More: If you have trouble focusing (or would simply like to learn more about this practice), try either the Calm or Headspace apps, which provide specific prompts that you can use to create a relaxed state of mind.

#12. Write in a Journal (or with "Morning Pages")

In her book *The Artist's Way*, Julia Cameron invites readers to begin each day with what she calls "Morning Pages." As Cameron explains on her blog,

> Morning Pages are three pages of longhand, stream of consciousness writing, done first thing in the morning. There is no wrong way to do Morning Pages – they are not high art. They are not even "writing." They are about anything and everything that crosses your mind – and they are for your eyes only. Morning Pages provoke, clarify, comfort, cajole, prioritize and synchronize the day at hand.

Working through Morning Pages for ten minutes is an excellent mindfulness habit because you completely focus on putting your thoughts onto paper. It's a way to liberate your mind from the mental chatter that can set your morning off to a negative or anxious start.

Further, the act of writing in longhand, which is a must for Morning Pages, adds to the experience of being present. Handwriting forces you to slow down, to think about what you're writing, and it engages more areas of the brain than typing.

If writing Morning Pages feels too unstructured for you, you can write in a journal about specific topics of your choosing or use journal prompts. Like Morning Pages, journaling brings your wandering mind to attention by actively engaging with your thoughts.

Journaling can help you focus on your inner world, your goals, and even your nightly dreams. (If you're interested in journaling, Steve has a detailed post about this habit on his blog.)

Action Plan: Buy a few spiral notebooks or journals in addition to quality writing pens that flow well on paper.

Start by deciding where you want to write. It could be sitting in your bed, as soon as you awaken. Or you may need a shower and a cup of coffee before you are clearheaded enough to begin. Just be sure your notebook and pen are visible and readily available in your writing spot.

Take a few deep breaths with your eyes closed, and then simply begin writing. For Morning Pages, simply write whatever comes into your head. It doesn't need to make sense or have any particular purpose. But if it does, that's fine too.

If you decide to focus on more directed journal writing, decide on the type of journaling you wish to do. You might want to write in:

- » A dream journal,
- » A gratitude journal,
- » A relationship journal,
- » A prayer journal,
- » Or you can even draw or doodle in your journal.

You can use journal prompts that you create for yourself or that you find online. Barrie uses the prompt, "What do I need to know today?" Then she waits for ideas or thoughts to arise that she writes down in her journal.

You can be as creative or simple as you wish with your Morning Pages or journaling. The purpose is to spend ten mindful minutes with pen in hand, writing down the contents of your mind—whether the thoughts are directed or stream of consciousness.

Once the ten minutes is up, finish the sentence you are writing or the thought you want to capture, and close your journal. Save what you have written to read at a later date. Allowing some time to go by before you read your journal entry can shed some additional light on the meaning of your writing.

Learn More: To learn more about Morning Pages, read Julia Cameron's book *The Artist's Way*, as well as her companion book, *The Miracle of Morning Pages: Everything You Always Wanted to Know about the Most Important Artist's Way Tool*

Check out the book *365 Journal Writing Ideas* by Rossi Fox for a year's worth of journal writing ideas, prompts, and actions. *Start Where You Are: A Journal for Self-Exploration* by Meera Lee Patel is another beautifully illustrated journal that includes prompts and exercises along with inspirational quotes to encourage reflection through writing, drawing, chart-making, and more.

You can also find many sites online with free journal writing prompts, like this one at Journaling Sage.

#13. Read Inspirational Content

Do you keep your phone or computer by your bedside table and check your emails or the news as soon as you awaken?

Maybe you turn on the television as soon as you get out of bed to catch up on the morning news, most of which is negative and agitating.

Rather than beginning your day with information overload, you can choose to read uplifting, inspiring, and positive books or articles.

Over the years, Steve and Barrie have read hundreds of self-improvement and motivational books. Some of their most profound "aha" insights have come as a result of what they have learned from these amazing books.

We firmly believe you should never stop learning and growing as a person. In fact, an important part of being a mindful person includes challenging your own beliefs and assumptions and reading the ideas and perspectives of others in order to stretch yourself.

This requires a proactive decision to read books that uplift and educate you and support your values, goals, and passions.

Says award-winning author Anne Lamott in her bestselling book *Bird by Bird*, "What a miracle it is that out of these small, flat, rigid squares of paper unfolds world after world after world, worlds that sing to you, comfort and quiet or excite you. Books help us understand who we are and how we are to behave. They show us what community and friendship mean; they show us how to live and die."

You might choose a spiritual reading, a book of daily quotations, or a personal growth book that encourages or motivates you. You might select a biography of someone you find inspirational and compelling or a novel that stokes your curiosity.

You don't have to read just books to find inspiration in the morning. There are plenty of blogs and websites that feature uplifting articles and quotes. Steve's site, Develop Good Habits, and Barrie's site,

Live Bold and Bloom, have hundreds of articles on a variety of self-improvement topics.

Whatever you decide to read, it should be engaging enough to keep your attention for at least ten minutes and powerful enough to make you want to read longer. You also want to reflect on what you are reading and allow the ideas to seep into your consciousness and stir your emotions in an elevating way.

Action Plan: Decide what kind of reading would provide positive feelings and inspiration for you. Find a book that meets your personal goals and that you find inspiring in some way.

Consider purchasing a paperback version of the book so you can underline or highlight passages that are meaningful to you. Or you could read a book on the Kindle platform, highlight important pages in your e-reading device, and then use the use a tool called Clippings.io to upload your notes to a tool like Evernote.

Next, think about where you want to do your reading.

> » In your bed upon first awakening?
> » At the kitchen table while you drink coffee?
> » In a special chair in a quiet space in your house?

Wherever you decide to do your reading, be sure you keep the book and a pen or highlighter handy.

Before you open the book, close your eyes and take a few deep, cleansing breaths to clear your mind and calm yourself. Get into a mental space for engaging with the material you're about to read.

As you read, try to focus intently on the words and their meaning for you. Read slowly and deliberately, taking moments to absorb and reflect on the positive thoughts being shared.

If you want, make notes about what you're reading in a journal or in the margins of the book. Write down any changes you want to make, actions you're inspired to take, or insights you've discovered through your reading.

Once you finish reading, take a few more deep breaths before you continue with your morning activities.

Learn More

Some of Barrie's favorite inspirational books include:

- » *The Power of Now* and *A New Earth* by Eckhart Tolle
- » *Way of the Peaceful Warrior* by Dan Millman
- » *Mindset: The New Psychology of Success* by Carol Dweck
- » *Loving What Is* by Byron Katie
- » *A Year of Living Consciously: 365 Daily Inspirations for Creating a Life of Passion and Purpose* by Gay Hendricks, PhD
- » *The How of Happiness* by Sonja Lyubomirsky, PhD

Some of Steve's favorite inspirational books include:

- » *Replay* by Ken Grimwood
- » *The Success Principles* by Jack Canfield
- » *Deep Work* by Cal Newport
- » *The Power of Less* by Leo Babauta
- » *Focal Point* by Brian Tracy
- » *The Joy of Less* by Francine Jay

» *The Slight Edge* by Jeff Olson
» *The One Thing* by Gary Keller and Jay Papasan

Finally, here is a list of 110 self-improvement books to choose from in various categories.

#14. Set a Daily Intention

Think about the difference between the following two statements:

» I plan to finish my project by 3:00 today.
» I intend to finish my project by 3:00 today.

Which statement is more powerful? Which one makes you believe that the person making the statement is more likely to follow through?

Of course, *to intend* to do something has more potency than *to plan* to do it. **Intention implies determination, will, and resolve.** There's a boldness to an intention that a plan can never muster.

When you set a daily intention, you resolve to make it happen, come hell or high water. You are determined to prioritize this action or mind-set to the exclusion of other activities in order to assure you make it happen.

Intentions give you a sense of purpose, as well as the inspiration and motivation to achieve your purpose.

An intention is the fuel behind all of your dreams and goals, the ones that are most valuable and important to you. The classic Hindu text known as the *Upanishads* declares, "You are what your deepest desire is. As your desire is, so is your intention. As your intention is, so is your will. As your will is, so is your deed. As your deed is, so is your destiny."

By setting a daily intention, you laser-focus on your deepest desires and what you will do today to bring them to fruition. Your intention can be a complete goal in itself, or it can be an action toward a bigger or more long-term goal.

Says author and spiritual teacher Deepak Chopra, "Only when you release your intentions into the fertile depths of your consciousness can they grow and flourish."

Action Plan: Your job with a daily intention is to plant it into the depths of your consciousness first thing in the morning.

The first step in setting your intention for the day is deciding what part of your life the intention will focus on.

You can set intentions around:

- » your mental or emotional state for the day
- » the quality of your relationships
- » your connection with God or the divine
- » your behavioral choices
- » a specific small goal, like exercising or smiling more often
- » a larger, long-term goal that involves daily actions

Once you decide on the type of intention you want to create, then write down your intention using words that are positive and manageable.

For example, you might write:

- » I intend to listen more carefully to my spouse without interrupting.
- » I intend to let inner peace be my guide today with all of my decisions.
- » I intend to complete three pages of my novel.

If your intention involves tangible steps (e.g., setting a specific time, gathering tools, etc.), then also write down the steps you'll need to take today to follow through on your intention.

After you write down your intention, speak it out loud in a clear, confident voice, looking at yourself in the mirror. Then close your eyes and say it again silently to yourself. Follow this by taking a few deep breaths as you allow your words of intention to sink into your consciousness.

Learn More: For more ideas and inspiration on using intention, check Wayne Dyer's bestselling book *The Power of Intention: Learning to Co-create Your World Your Way*. Also check out *The Intention Experiment: Using Your Thoughts to Change Your Life and the World* by Lynne McTaggart.

#15. Define Three Daily Goals

One of your intentions can be to accomplish three goals for the day—one in the morning, one at midday, and one in the late afternoon or evening.

Of course, you can set these three goals without using an intention, and the benefit will be the same: you'll define three important activities you want to achieve for the day and determine a way to get them done.

Why three goals?

Because three is a manageable number.

Rather than writing a to-do list of twenty or more items, make it simple. Narrow your list to the top three that you know with certainty you can achieve during the day. You can always do more, as long as you achieve your top three.

Having just three goals also allows you the time and mental energy to focus on them mindfully and thoroughly, without pressure to rush through each action in order to get to the next one. Taking your time with each goal allows you to enjoy the process of completing them.

Also, spending a few minutes to set your goals for the day and write them down allows you to be more creative, proactive, and thoughtful about how you structure your day and what you accomplish.

Says Winifred Gallagher, author of *Rapt: Attention and the Focused Life*, "Indeed, your ability to focus on this and suppress that is the key to controlling your experience and, ultimately, your well-being."

With these three goals defined first thing in the morning, you will be less likely to be distracted and pulled away by other activities that don't serve your larger goals and intentions.

Action Plan: Consider keeping a goals notebook, journal, or app on your phone or computer.

Decide when and where you want to determine your three daily goals. You might want to do this before you get out of bed upon awakening, or maybe you need to wake up your brain with a shower and cup of coffee before you can think about your daily goals.

Make sure you don't have any distractions for the ten minutes you work on these goals. Close your door, turn off your phone, and settle in to a quiet space.

Before you begin pondering your goals, close your eyes and take a few deep, cleansing breaths.

Then begin by writing down everything you want to accomplish for the entire week. Conduct a brain dump of every possible goal you can think of. You may have a list of twenty to thirty action items (or more). You can use this master list throughout the week (adding to it if necessary) to choose your daily goals.

Review the list to determine any that you feel you must accomplish today. Perhaps they have a deadline or you've been putting them off for too long. You may have more than three of these must-do goals, but pick the top three for now. If they are all equal in priority, then choose three randomly.

Make sure each of the three goals is achievable within a couple of hours or less. If the goals are too large, you'll feel overwhelmed and disappointed because they take too long.

Break down larger goals into smaller actions, and make those smaller actions separate daily goals. Also, write down the time of day you want to work on each goal.

If you are new to setting daily goals, start with three very small and easy goals like:

1. Pay one of my bills.
2. Clean out the cat box.
3. Send a birthday card to Mom.

Just the act of setting, then accomplishing your goals, no matter how small and easy, will give you a boost of confidence.

After you complete your daily goals, return to your goals notebook and cross them off. Each morning before you define your daily goals, review all that you've accomplished, and take a moment to celebrate.

Learn More: If you'd like to improve on your goal-setting efforts, you can check out Steve's book, *S.M.A.R.T. Goals Made Simple - 10 Steps to Master Your Personal and Career Goals.*

#16. Visualize Your Daily Goals

Novak Djokovic, a Serbian professional tennis player who is currently ranked number two in the world, says he regularly uses visualization to prepare for a match, overcome self-doubt, and recover more quickly from mistakes, helping him become one of the greatest comeback players of all time.

Olympic swimmer Michael Phelps, the most decorated Olympian in history, has been using visualization since he was a small child. During the Olympics and before any race, he visualizes every minute detail of his performance and credits this mindfulness practice for his competitive edge.

Visualization doesn't just enhance athletic performance. It can be used in daily life to relieve stress and performance anxiety, enhance preparation, and add more power to your physical and mental efforts.

Visualization has been shown to impact motor control, attention, perception, planning, and memory, priming your brain for success in whatever you want to accomplish.

The simple act of visualizing, which requires mindfulness, focus, and creativity, frees the mind from mental chatter and negativity.

By using visualization, you create strong neural pathways in your brain, just as if you had actually performed what you visualize. Because the brain tells the muscles how to move, these neural pathways result in more precise, stronger movements, enhancing your actual efforts.

Begin your day with a ten-minute visualization exercise, and you can supercharge your goals and desired outcomes. Visualizing activates your creative subconscious, allowing you to generate more creative ideas to achieve your goals.

Action Plan: Here are seven steps to practice visualization in the morning:

1. **Define your goal or outcome.** Before you visualize what you want, define your goal or desired outcome. It needs to be specific, detailed, and achievable. Visualizing your three daily goals or your daily intention is a good way to start.

2. **Define the actions for achievement.** Write down the specific actions you'll take to achieve your goal. Outline these steps before you begin your visualization practice so you know

exactly what you want to visualize yourself doing.

3. **Decide on your visualization time.** Determine when during your morning routine you want to practice visualizing. If you include setting three goals or an intention as part of your morning habits, then right after you set the goals or intention, visualize yourself accomplishing them.

4. **Prepare yourself.** Be sure you're in a quiet space without distractions. Sit comfortably and take a few deep breaths to quiet your mind and to get into a more meditative state. Then mentally picture a blank slate. From that blank slate, begin your visualization. If other thoughts arise, gently turn your attention back to your visualization, just as you would with meditation.

5. **Begin with the outcome.** As you visualize, picture yourself reaching the goal first. Visualize it as if it were a movie and you are the lead character. Picture exactly what you are doing, how you look, who is around you, where you are, and how you feel. Get as specific and detailed as possible.

6. **Visualize the actions.** After you visualize reaching your goal, mentally rehearse the details of each action you need to take to make it happen. If your goal has many mental steps and actions involved in making it happen (like finding a new job), then visualize successfully completing the actions required for the day. Allow yourself to be immersed in these mental pictures, as though you are actually experiencing what you visualize.

7. **Go back to the outcome.** To end the visualization session, see yourself reaching the desired goal once again. Notice how you feel having accomplished this goal in your mind's eye. Take a few deep breaths and open your eyes to begin your day.

Learn More: If you'd like to learn more about the power of visualization, check out *Creative Visualization: Use the Power of Your Imagination to Create What You Want in Your Life* by Shakti Gawain. We also recommend *Healing Visualizations: Creating Health Through Imagery* by Gerald Epstein, MD, and *The Art of Mental Training – A Guide to Performance Excellence* by DC Gonzalez.

#17. Create a Tea or Coffee Ritual

For most of us, that morning cup of coffee or tea is a means to an end rather than a mindfulness exercise. We need that shot of caffeine to get us moving and awake.

Rather than stumbling to the coffee maker or teapot in a sleepy haze and slugging down that first cup, you can create a morning ceremony around this daily habit.

Says Jesse Jacobs, owner of Samovar Tea Lounge in San Francisco, "Rituals slow us down and connect us to this moment here and now. I'm not talking about big, ornate cultural or religious rituals. Instead I'm referring to simple actions that connect us to ourselves, our place, and the present moment."

Ritualized tea ceremonies have been practiced in Asian cultures for centuries, and similar tea drinking habits can be found worldwide, from Great Britain to Morocco. These rituals involve savoring and fully experiencing every aspect of preparing and drinking a cup of tea.

This ritual doesn't have to be limited to tea. You can also make a ritual of your morning coffee, as it can involve similar steps in preparation. In fact, Ethiopians have ritualized coffee preparation in the same way Asians have for tea.

But you don't need to follow any ancient traditional ceremony to enjoy your own morning ritual. All you really need to do is slow down, pay attention, and savor.

Action Plan: Start by purchasing some fresh, loose tea leaves or freshly roasted coffee beans. If you don't have a tea strainer or bean grinder, you can use what you have, but starting with fresh ingredients makes the ceremony (and the experience) of drinking more pleasurable.

For tea drinkers ...

Begin by selecting your favorite teacup or mug, one that makes you happy. Hold it in your hands and make sure you like the way it feels.

Pull out your tins of loose tea or your tea bags, and smell each one. Allow each scent to "speak" to you. Which tea matches your mood or state of mind? Select your tea and place it in a teapot, cup, or strainer.

Next, put water in an open pot on the stove and watch it heat up and boil. Watch the steam rise and bubbles form in the pan. Practice mindful breathing as you watch and wait.

When the water boils, slowly pour the water over the tea leaves or tea bag. Watch as the leaves swirl and the water begins to change color as the tea infuses it.

Decide where you want to drink your tea. Find a quiet, calm place where you can focus on the tea without interruption or distraction.

Before you take the first sip, bring the cup to your lips, feel the warm steam, and notice the complex aromas. Take a sip as though you were tasting tea for the first time.

Notice the sweetness or bitterness of the tea. Notice the delicacy or robustness. Hold the tea in your mouth for a moment and then swallow it reverently.

Hold the cup in your hands, feeling the warmth of the cup and enjoying the sensations of that first sip. Continue to take sips like this, slowly and thoughtfully, savoring each sip with gratitude.

End the ritual by washing out the cup, drying it, and putting it away.

For coffee drinkers …

You can follow the same steps, focusing on grinding the coffee beans (or putting ground coffee in the coffee maker) and brewing the coffee.

You might consider a "pour over" coffee that requires you to slowly pour boiling water over the grounds through a filter, directly into your cup. Barrie uses an electric gooseneck kettle made for this purpose.

Learn More: If tea ceremonies interest you, read *The Book of Tea* by Kakuzo Okakura with an introduction by American tea writer Bruce Richardson.

One line from Okakura's book offers an enticing summary: "The heaven of modern humanity is indeed shattered in the Cyclopean struggle for wealth and power … Meanwhile, let us have a sip of tea."

Also take a look at this list of blogs about tea drinking, as well as the Samovar Tea Lounge blog.

For coffee lovers, check out *The World Atlas of Coffee: From Beans to Brewing — Coffees Explored, Explained and Enjoyed* by James Hoffmann.

#18. Eat Breakfast Mindfully

Remember how your mom would nag you to eat breakfast when you were a kid, hammering home that, "It's the most important meal of the day"?

Although recent studies don't support your mom's advice, eating breakfast does raise the body's energy level and restores the blood glucose level to normal after an overnight fast.

If you eat breakfast, even if it is something simple like a piece of toast or a cup of yogurt, then consider making breakfast a mindful activity.

Rather than eating on the go and unconsciously grabbing something just to fill your stomach, make breakfast a mini-celebration to get your day off to a happy, healthy start.

Mindful eating involves both what you eat and how you eat it. Being mindful about your breakfast is a great way to reevaluate your food choices while slowing down enough to appreciate what you are eating. Eating healthy foods at breakfast can set the stage for smart food choices throughout your day.

Action Plan: If you are sticking to the ten-minute plan, you'll need to choose foods you can prepare and sit down to eat during this time. That doesn't mean eating doughnuts or Pop-Tarts just because they are quick and easy.

You can still prepare and eat a healthy breakfast in ten minutes, especially if you make sure you have everything you need the night before.

Some ideas for quick, mindful, and healthy breakfasts include:

» a scrambled egg, a piece of whole grain toast, and some fruit

» a bowl of quick-cook oatmeal with bananas and walnuts

» a banana and peanut butter smoothie

» an egg white omelet with shredded cheese and salsa

» Greek yogurt topped with muesli and berries

As you prepare your food, be attentive and present. Notice what you are cooking and how the food looks and smells. Notice your own feelings of hunger as you prepare the food.

Set a place at your table, as though you are your own honored guest for breakfast. Set a place for others in your family if they are joining you.

As you eat, pay attention to:

» how the food smells and looks on your plate

» the various tastes of the food as you try each bite

» how full (or sated) you are before, during, and after eating

» your emotions during and after eating

» where the food came from and who produced it

Once you finish eating, take a moment to reflect with gratitude that you had this healthy food to nourish you. Wash your plate, dry it, and put it away.

Learn More: If you want to learn more about mindful eating, read *Savor: Mindful Eating, Mindful Life* by Thích Nhất Hạnh, as well as *Mindful Eating: A Guide to Rediscovering a Healthy and Joyful Relationship with Food* by Jan Chozen Bays, MD.

You might also enjoy this *New York Times* article called "Mindful Eating As Food for Thought."

#19. Be Present with Your Family

In the scenario described in the beginning of this book, our erstwhile hero races into the kitchen, only to encounter his frazzled family members dealing with their own cycles of unconsciousness.

Rather than engage in the chaos, he rushes out the door, bagel in hand, to charge off to work with just a hasty "good-bye" to his spouse and kids.

How many families in how many households around the world begin their days with little to no interaction with the people they hold most dear? What are we working so hard for anyway, if not to spend quality time with our loved ones?

Mindfulness habits in a family must be taught and modeled by at least one adult member of the family. You can be a role model for your spouse and your children on the importance of mindfulness, particularly in your relationships.

The best place to start is by showing them the power of being present, even for just a few minutes before you begin your work or school day.

Action Plan: Being present with someone means you are fully attentive and focused on the other person. You aren't looking at your phone, distracted by the television, or thinking about the next thing you need to do.

Mornings are usually pretty hectic, so it's easy to rush around and make a quick exit instead of truly connecting with your family members. That's why you should consider carving out *just* ten minutes in the morning that are devoted entirely to one or all of your family members.

One of the best ways to be present with your family is by sitting down together for breakfast. You can ask your children or spouse questions about their day ahead or any other topic and listen without judgment.

Share an inspirational reading or topic that you all discuss, or simply listen attentively to what your family members are sharing at the table. Be sure to create a "no phone, no computer" policy at the table.

If you don't have time for a family breakfast, try to make a personal connection with one or more of your family members. You can take a short walk, spend a few moments on a project together, or just look them in the eye, offer a long hug and kiss, and say, "I love you." Sit with your spouse or a child on the couch and just hug one another for a few minutes.

Express love and appreciation to each of your family members every morning, and let them know how much you value them.

Learn More: For more information on teaching your children mindfulness practices, read *Growing Up Mindful: Essential Practices to Help Children, Teens, and Families Find Balance, Calm, and Resilience* by Christopher Willard.

Also, check out this article called "8 Ways to be Powerfully Present with Your Family."

#20. Practice Family Meditation

Over the last several years, there has been an explosion of interest in school-based mindfulness programs offered to children and youth in the United States.

Research studies of these programs show the profound effect meditation and other mindfulness practices have on a child's academic performance, self-esteem, and empathy.

According to one study of the Oakland-based Mindful Schools program, "student behavior improved significantly in all four areas measured—paying attention, self-control, classroom participation, and respect for others—and these gains were maintained seven weeks later."

Practicing a ten-minute meditation with your children in the mornings not only helps them succeed in school, but it also provides another opportunity for closeness and presence within your family.

Teaching your children the skills to fend off negative thoughts and behaviors, improve focus, boost their confidence, and treat others and themselves with respect and compassion is a tool that will serve them for the rest of their lives. Sharing meditation with your kids will also reinforce your own practice.

Action Plan: How you meditate with your children will differ based on the ages of your kids. Young children will have a harder time staying quiet and focused, so you'll need to adapt your practice to your child's abilities.

Older children and teens can better understand what meditation is, but they may be more resistant or dismissive of the idea.

For young children ...

Explain to them in very simple terms what meditation is (sitting quietly and paying attention to breathing) and why it's important (it makes your mind stronger).

Begin with a very short amount of time, maybe two or three minutes to start, especially for preschoolers.

Show your child how to breathe from the stomach by expanding it on the inhalation. Then have him or her breathe as you softly count down from ten to one, counting on the exhalation. Try this countdown a few times, for as long as your child can remain quiet and still.

Another way to practice meditation with your child is by candle gazing. Sit at a table with your child and light a candle in the center of the table. Set a timer for two or three minutes and ask your child to simply gaze at the flame without talking or looking around.

Make your meditation time fun so your child will see it as a game rather than a chore. Find a way to reward your child as he or she increases time in meditation. Create a meditation calendar, and give your child a gold star for every morning he or she meditates with you.

For older children and teens ...

Discuss the benefits of meditation and why you want to create a morning practice as a family. If you meet resistance, ask your child to give it a try for a few days. Show them this list of celebrities who meditate regularly.

Explain a basic breathing meditation to your children, using diaphragmatic breathing and counting down from ten.

Find a comfortable, quiet space where your family can sit in meditation. Begin the meditation time by inviting your family to take a few deep, cleansing breaths. You can use a bell to begin the meditation time if you like.

You might consider using an audio guided meditation or a meditation app on your phone to help your child stay focused and engaged. (Again, the Calm or Headspace apps are good starting points because they provide specific prompts that you and your family can follow.)

End the meditation time by holding hands with your family and having a moment of connection before you begin the activities of the day.

Learn More: Check out this article from The Chopra Center on three kid-friendly meditations.

If you are interested in teaching your child more about meditation and mindfulness, read the book *Growing Up Mindful: Essential Practices to Help Children, Teens, and Families Find Balance, Calm, and Resilience* by Christopher Willard.

Finally, **Steve recorded a walkthrough video of the Headspace app that you can watch as part of the free companion website**.

#21. Connect with Nature

On a busy morning, the only time you might spend outside is the short walk from your house to your car. But taking a few minutes out of your morning routine to spend outside can have a profound effect on your mental and physical well-being.

Numerous studies have shown that spending time in nature can boost your immune system, relieve symptoms of depression and anxiety, improve concentration and creativity, relieve stress, and improve your memory.

Even if you live in a city, you will benefit from fresh air (hopefully) and a few minutes of paying attention to the elements of nature you observe, from the birds flying overhead to the sound of the wind.

Action Plan: Pick a quiet spot in your yard or near your house that you find relaxing and appealing. Make it a place where you won't be interrupted by neighbors or passing cars.

You can stand or sit—whatever feels more comfortable to you. Then take a few deep, cleansing breaths.

Begin to pay full attention to your surroundings using all of your senses. Listen attentively to the sounds around you—the wind in the leaves, the birds singing, the neighbor's wind chimes.

Notice the clouds moving across the sky, the leaves blowing on the ground, the squirrels chasing one another.

Take a deep breath and notice the smells, whether it's the lingering aroma of a rain shower or the fragrance of flowers in your garden.

Touch the bark of a tree or run your hand through the damp grass.

Close your eyes and allow yourself to be fully present in gratitude for nature and your connection to it.

Learn More: If you want to enhance your practice of mindfulness in nature, read this article called "Why Meditating in Nature Is Easier."

When you can't be outside in nature, try this three-hour Zen Meditation Music with nature sounds that you can use while working or studying.

#22. Complete a 10-Minute Exercise Warm-Up

We don't need to explain the benefits of exercise. They are numerous and compelling. Even so, most people don't have a regular fitness routine. They view exercise as a chore and find a myriad of excuses to avoid it, even while they long for the benefits they know it provides.

One reason we avoid exercise is the way we view it—as a means to an end rather than an enjoyable activity on its own. Exercise can easily become a mindfulness activity if you shift your thoughts about how you approach it.

If you see it as a way to connect with your body and become more aware of your own physical abilities, you can lessen some of your resistance to it.

For many people, simply initiating exercise for just a few minutes is enough to get the ball rolling. Just beginning anything you mentally resist is 95% of the battle.

If you don't have time for a full exercise routine in the morning, just devote ten minutes to moving and warming up your body to get your blood and energy flowing.

This ten-minute mindfulness exercise habit might be enough to kick-start a regular fitness routine for thirty minutes to an hour a day.

Action Plan: Take a few deep, cleansing breaths. Then notice how your body feels. Are you experiencing any pain or discomfort? Without reacting to the feelings, simply identify them.

As you perform each of the following exercises, imagine sending energy to the part or parts of your body performing the work.

As you engage in the movements of your exercise, find an anchor to hold your focus. You might focus at something out the window or an object in the room.

Be sure you continue to breathe as you perform each exercise. You might want to use breathing as your anchor to help you remember.

The exercises:

Start by doing two minutes of marching in place to warm up your muscles.

Next, pick up the pace by doing two minutes of jumping jacks. If you need to, you can modify these to low-impact jacks (moving your arms up and down but simply extending each leg to the side instead of jumping).

Then move to doing a series of squats for one minute. Stand with your feet slightly wider than your hips. Put your arms straight in front of you, and keep your spine in a neutral position.

Breathe in, break at your hips and push your butt back. Keep sending your hips backward as your knees begin to bend. Focus on keeping your knees in line with your feet, and squat down until your hip joint is lower than your knees (if you can go that far). Modify if necessary.

Next, jog in place or do a high knee march for two minutes.

Follow with one minute of lunges, either moving or in place. Start in a split stance. Your front knee should move forward as little as possible and should never pass your toes. Drive your hips straight back up to come out of the lunge.

End the ten-minute routine by marching in place again, followed by a few more deep breaths.

Learn More: If you'd like to see a simple warm-up routine, then check out this 5-minute workout video on YouTube.

#23. Do a Sun Salutation Yoga Routine

Yoga is an excellent mindfulness practice that helps you create balance in the body through stretching and flexibility, and awareness in the mind through concentration on poses.

Research has shown that yoga provides a variety of mental and physical health benefits, helping reduce stress, improve mood, reduce inflammation, and increase energy.

Just like meditation, yoga has many styles of practices with different exercises, philosophies, and desired outcomes. Most practices include physical poses (asanas) designed to purify the body and provide physical strength and stamina.

Yoga works with the energy in the body, through pranayama or energy-control, as well as breath-control in order to still the mind and attain higher states of awareness.

Action Plan: There are so many possibilities for a short morning yoga practice, but we like the sun salutation (or surya namaskar in Sanskrit) as a way to begin the practice.

Most yoga classes begin with several repetitions of a sun salutation as a warm-up and to help with focus as you begin the class.

A sun salutation provides a great stretch for your entire body, as it strengthens your arms, shoulders, and legs.

There are many ways to perform a sun salutation, but we will share a very simple nine-step process to get you started:

1. Using a yoga mat or standing on a rug, **begin in mountain pose** with your feet hip-width apart and your arms at your sides. Look straight ahead and make sure your weight is evenly distributed between both feet. Inhale and exhale evenly through your nose.

2. Hold your hands together in a prayer position in front of your heart, and then set an intention for your yoga practice, such as "I intend to release negative thoughts." Inhale and raise your hands toward the ceiling with your arms straight in an **upward salute**. Gently arch your back as you look up toward your hands.

3. Exhale and bend over at the waist into a **standing forward bend**, keeping your back straight. Place your palms flat on the floor next to either foot. Your fingers should point forward and be fully spread apart so that your entire palm is pressing into the floor. If you can't reach the floor, stack books or blocks for your hands to rest on.

4. Inhale and extend your spine into a **standing half forward bend**, which allows you to move more easily into a four-limbed staff pose in which you lower your body to the floor, resting on your stomach. Lift your head and shoulders, using your upper arms to support you. Your arms are bent, and your upper arms should be parallel to the floor.

5. Transition to **upward facing dog** by pushing up with your arms and pressing your hands into the floor, and then gently arch your back, open your chest, and look up at the ceiling.

6. Exhale and roll back over your toes so that your body ends up in an inverted "V" shape with your legs straight and palms on the floor. This pose is called **downward facing dog.** Keep your palms pressed to the floor and your abs engaged.

7. After five breaths in downward dog, bend your knees to your chest and step forward into the half-standing forward bend. Then exhale and bend completely forward into standing forward bend from Step 3.

8. Inhale and rise completely into the upward salute from Step 2.

9. Bring your prayer hands back to your sides as you exhale and return to the mountain pose from Step 1. You have come full circle with your sun salutation.

Learn More: The best way to learn the sun salutation is by watching it performed. You can find dozens of videos online showing you the sun salutation, but we like this one that gives you options based on your flexibility and strength.

If you are interested in starting a yoga practice, try the Yoga For Beginners (by Body Wisdom) DVD or Rodney Yee's Am/Pm Yoga for Beginners, both of which can be found on Amazon.com.

#24. Recite Positive Affirmations

Those things we repeatedly say to ourselves out loud or in our thoughts are affirmations, whether they are disparaging or encouraging words.

As a mindfulness habit, affirmations are *positive phrases* that you repeat to yourself, describing who and how you want to be, using the present tense, as though the outcome has already occurred.

As you repeat the phrase, you are present with the reality of it just as though it were already true. Establishing a positive affirmation habit first thing in the morning can impact the outcome of your entire day.

Used this way, affirmations can change the way we view the world and even influence our actions. Neuroscience now proves that our thoughts can change the structure and function of our brains.

Positive affirmations, when practiced deliberately and repeatedly, can reinforce chemical pathways in the brain, making the connection between two neurons stronger, and therefore more likely to conduct the same message again.

A brain scan imaging study showed that using positive self-affirmation activates the parts of our brains involved in expecting and receiving a reward, reinforcing the likelihood that positive change will occur.

Action Plan: When creating affirmations, focus on what you want, not on what you don't want. Rather than saying, "I don't want to be lonely anymore," you might say, "I have many loving and fulfilling relationships." Remember to use the present tense.

As you decide on your daily or weekly affirmative statement, consider where you need the most change or support in your life. *A relationship? Your self-image? Your professional success?* You might consider choosing a "theme" for the week related to this issue and create several related affirmations to repeat during each session.

Stand in front of a mirror and speak to yourself out loud in a clear, strong, and confident voice, saying affirmative positive statements that encourage and inspire you.

Begin by repeating your affirmations for two to three minutes. If you want to reinforce your verbal statements, write them down in a journal as well.

Here are a number of examples:

- » *"I am in control of my life."*
- » *"I am worthy of love and joy."*
- » *"I can make a change in this world."*
- » *"I embrace my uniqueness, which makes me beautiful, body and soul."*
- » *"I will accomplish my goals today."*
- » *"I am brimming with energy. I am active and alive."*

» *"I possess the qualities needed to be successful."*

» *"Abundance and blessings flow freely through me."*

» *"Every decision I make is the right one for me."*

» *"I take pleasure and satisfaction in my own solitude."*

» *"I breathe in calmness and breathe out nervousness."*

» *"I let go of my anger so I can see clearly. I am in charge of how I feel."*

» *"Today is a positive, calm, and productive day."*

» *"I approve of myself and love myself deeply and completely."*

» *"Every day I am more confident and happy."*

» *"I know what I want, and I'm not afraid to go after it."*

As you speak the affirmations, say them in the way you would say them to a beloved friend or child. Speak to your reflection in a way that is sincere and loving. Don't just speak the words in a rote manner without belief or feeling.

One option is instead of using the word "I" in your affirmation, try speaking to yourself in the third person, using your own name. For example, you might say, "Jenny, you are becoming more and more confident at work every day."

Psychologist Ethan Kross of the University of Michigan found in his research that employing "a subtle linguistic shift — shifting from 'I' to your own name — can have really powerful self-regulatory effects."

This shift can help you step outside of your internal musings and speak from the voice of your "higher self."

Learn More: If you need some ideas for affirmations, **take a look at the list of the affirmations that Barrie has included on the**

companion website.

Also, you might enjoy the 64 *Power Thought Cards* by Louise Hay, author of the international bestseller *You Can Heal Your Life*, which you can find on Amazon or on her website.

#25. Declutter One Space

It's easy to become attached to things, routines, and environments. We allow our homes to become repositories for every new whim, and we accumulate more and more stuff over the years. Then our lives get so busy that we don't have time to enjoy or organize the stuff we've accumulated.

If fact, our material possessions can contribute to our sense of overwhelm, stress, and emptiness, as we realize that "things" don't fulfill us in the way we hoped they might.

As we mention in our book *10-Minute Declutter*,

Clutter is often a reflection of our inner selves. If we feel disorganized, out of sorts, depressed, stressed out or insecure, it shows up in the way we manage our daily lives. Organizing your clutter is a path to healing emotional blocks and inner confusion. As you reclaim control over your stuff, you'll feel better about yourself and have more positive energy.

That's why adopting the habit of simplifying and organizing one space for ten minutes every day is such a powerful and life-changing endeavor.

If you maintain this habit, you can simplify your entire house and create a calm, peaceful environment that reinforces your other mindfulness habits.

Just the act of decluttering, which involves making value decisions about your possessions and letting some of them go, is a perfect mindfulness activity. You are forced to challenge your attachments and beliefs about the necessity of your stuff.

Action Plan: Pick one cluttered space in your house that has bothered you. Be sure it's a space that can be decluttered in a ten-minute time frame, like a drawer or desktop or one shelf of a closet. And be sure to have three boxes handy to use as you sort through the items in this space. Label them "Save," "Give Away," and "Throw Away."

Then do the following:

1. Remove everything from the space and set the items aside.
2. Clean or wipe down the space (the drawer, desktop, etc.), getting rid of dust and dirt so you can begin with a clean surface.
3. Begin sorting through the items you removed. Pull out everything you know you can give or throw away without hesitation, and sort those into the appropriate boxes.
4. Pull out any items you absolutely need or simply can't discard. If you are holding on to something because you feel guilty about letting it go, or you think you might need it someday (even though you haven't used it for years), reconsider putting the item in the discard or giveaway boxes.
5. For any items you feel "iffy" about, put them in the "Save" box.
6. Replace the things that you want to keep, organizing like items in a group. Find a way to store each category neatly and in a

way that is easily accessible, using boxes, bins, and containers you might have in your house. Be sure to label any containers that don't allow you to see the contents.

7. Empty your box of throwaway items in the trash, and put your box of giveaway items out of sight until you're ready to donate them. For things you want to save but not put back in the space, leave them in the "Save" box, label what's inside, and store them in a closet or storage space.

Step back, take a deep breath, and admire your clean, clutter-free, organized space. Pay attention to how this space and your efforts at decluttering it make you feel.

Learn More: You can declutter your entire home using the "10 Minute" strategy with our book *10 Minute Declutter: The Stress-Free Habit for Simplifying Your Home.*

PART IV

LATE-MORNING MINDFULNESS HABITS

#26. Practice Mindful Driving

According to a report in USA Today, the average American's commute to work is 25.5 minutes each way, which amounts to about 204 hours a year spent commuting.

If your morning routine involves driving to work, running errands, or taking your children to school, you know how "mindless" people can be in morning rush-hour traffic and how stressful driving in your car can be.

A 2014 *Time* magazine article highlights the negative impact this time in your car has on your mental and physical health. It's associated with:

- » higher blood sugar
- » higher cholesterol
- » increased risk of depression
- » increased anxiety
- » blood pressure spikes
- » back pain
- » a decrease in life satisfaction and happiness

As a result, people tend to do and say things in their cars that they wouldn't consider saying in another setting.

Says Jerry Kennard in an article for *Health Central*, "Sitting in a car is incompatible with stress build up. There is no physical outlet. We can't fight and we can't run, so tension simply builds with no obvious outlet."

If you know that driving causes you to feel anger, stress, and anxiety, then you can change your viewpoint of this task by practicing mindfulness.

Action Plan: When you get into your car, take a few deep breaths. Before you start to drive, pay attention to your body and any tension you might feel. Feel your hands on the steering wheel, the way your body feels on the seat, and the weight of your foot on the pedal.

Don't turn on the radio or create other distractions while in the car. Turn your phone on silent.

As you begin to drive, make an extra effort to notice your surroundings. Look at the houses, the trees, the other cars with people in them. Listen to the noises of your car, the wind, honking horns, etc. without judging or reacting.

Maybe try driving a bit slower or just below the speed limit, which can take away a good bit of tension.

If you get stuck in traffic or someone cuts you off, notice the feelings that arise (anger, frustration, anxiety, competitiveness), and simply identify them.

Use traffic stops or other necessary stops to practice a few deep, calming breaths. Notice what's around you—the sky, the buildings, the trees, and other people. Send a wish of loving compassion to the people you notice, saying to yourself, "May you be well, may you be happy."

Once you arrive at your destination, after you've turned off the engine, sit for a moment and take three deep breaths, really letting go on the exhalation.

Learn More: Read this article from *Everyday Mindfulness* about mindful driving. If you commute to work on a bus or subway, you'll enjoy this article about practicing mindfulness on your way to work.

#27. Practice Transition Breathing

If you've made it through your morning commute to your destination, whether it's to work or some other task or meeting, you need a transition to ease you into the day and the work you have before you.

How many times have you raced from your car into your office or work and immediately started doing something—checking emails, talking to coworkers, or jumping right into a project.

Of course it seems productive and diligent to get to work right away, but part of you is lagging behind, still processing the thoughts or feelings you carried in with you. Breathing helps to harness and quiet your thoughts.

David Gelles, author of *Mindful Work: How Meditation Is Changing Business from the Inside Out*, adds that, "We regain control of our attention. We come back to our breath over and over again even when our minds wander—and they're always wandering. Simple attention training can yield big benefits in the long run."

Allow yourself a mindful moment before you switch gears so you can approach your work in a more calm and centered way.

Action Plan: Once you walk into your destination, find a quiet place where you won't be interrupted for a few minutes. It might be your desk, or you may need to go to a bathroom stall and close the door.

Take a few deep, cleansing breaths. Then close your eyes and follow the breathing exercise you did for your morning breathing as follows:

» Inhale slowly until your lungs are filled to capacity. Breathe in through your nose, and gently push your stomach forward, as though you are filling your stomach.

» At the end of the inhalation, pause for a count of two.

» Exhale slowly, smoothly, and completely, and gently allow your stomach to return to its normal position. Pause at the end of the exhalation as well.

» When you first begin, don't take too full a breath at once. Start by breathing to the count of four, pausing for the count of two, and exhaling to the count of four.

» Keep your attention focused on the process of inhaling to the count of four, holding the breath for the count of two, and then exhaling for the count of four. If your mind wanders, gently bring it back to your breathing.

» Repeat the breathing cycle ten times or for just a few minutes if that's all the time you have.

» Take one more deep, cleansing breath before you begin your work.

Learn More: Read this *Harvard Business Review* article on "How to Practice Mindfulness Throughout Your Work Day," which includes a guided breathing exercise.

Also try this ten-minute guided breathing meditation on YouTube if you prefer a guided meditation.

#28. Clear Your Desk

We talked earlier about the mindfulness benefits of decluttering. Decluttering your desk or workspace is an important way to set the tone for mindfulness throughout your workday.

Visual clutter is distracting and agitating. It slows you down and makes you less productive. It impedes your creativity and clarity. It also sends a message to those around you that you are disorganized and scattered.

The act of clearing and organizing your desk allows you a few minutes of focused mindfulness, as you decide where to put your stuff and what to keep and throw away.

Once your desk is clear, you have set the stage for more mental and emotional energy and focus to begin your work.

Action Plan: If you have just a few moments to clear your desk before you begin a task or meeting, simply gather everything on your desktop and put it all in a drawer, box, or bag, leaving just what you need to start this project.

With ten minutes, however, you have time for some sorting and organizing. Follow the steps outlined in mindfulness habit #25 to sort, toss, and organize the items on your desktop.

You may need to file some papers, create new files, or take photos of documents to store on your phone so that you can toss the paper copy. It may be time to get rid of the knickknacks, books, and coffee mugs you've accumulated on your desk.

Once your desktop is clean and clear, take a deep breath and begin your work.

Learn More: Read this article by Joshua Becker of Becoming Minimalist called "The Simple Guide to a Clutter-Free Desk."

#29. Focus on Your Work Purpose

Why do you work? Of course you work to earn money so you can pay the bills. But why do you work at your particular job?

Says the Lebanese-American artist, poet, and writer Kahlil Gibran in his book *The Prophet*, "Work is love made visible." He states about work:

> It is to weave the cloth with threads drawn from your heart, even as if your beloved were to wear that cloth. It is to build a house with affection, even as if your beloved were to dwell in that house. It is to sow seeds with tenderness and reap the harvest with joy, even as if your beloved were to eat the fruit.

In other words, you should approach your work with love and purpose—no matter how challenging, uninspiring, or difficult it might be. To be mindful of the purpose of your work allows you to be more fully engaged with every task you perform.

Even if you hate your work, you can find a purpose for your efforts and reduce your feelings of negativity about your job and your life.

Action Plan: Before starting your first task, take a few deep, calming breaths to clear your mind.

Take a few minutes to think about why you work. At the most basic level, you work to provide for yourself and your family. You work so you can live in your home; drive your car; and have clothing, food, and other necessities, as well as many non-essentials that enrich your life.

If these are the only reasons you work, that's purpose enough. But work also provides a sense of accomplishment, productivity, and self-esteem.

If you truly enjoy your work, it provides fulfillment, passion, meaning, creative expression, and many other positive feelings.

Write down what you see as the purpose of your work. Close your eyes and focus on that purpose for a moment. See that purpose as the motivation and reason behind everything you plan to do in the day ahead.

Take a moment to consider what your life would be like without your work. How would it impact this purpose?

During this mindfulness exercise, don't allow cynicism or negativity about your work to infect this reflection on your work's purpose.

There will be other times to address any dissatisfaction you have with your work, which may be quite legitimate. For now, simply focus on your purpose and allow yourself to feel grateful and inspired.

Learn More: Check out this article in the *Harvard Business Review* about finding purpose in your work as an ongoing effort.

If you're interested in the science behind the power of purpose, check out the book Life on Purpose: How Living for What Matters Most Changes Everything by Victor J. Stretcher, PhD, MPH in which he explores "the connection between purposeful living and the latest scientific evidence on quality of life and longevity."

#30. Practice a Mindful Email Check-In

One of the more addictive behaviors we engage in is checking our email on our phones or computers. Most of us (Barrie included) will check our inboxes dozens of times a day, and it's a behavior that creates real stress and anxiety.

In fact, a research study revealed that checking and sending email at work can increase your blood pressure and heart rate and cause a spike in levels of the stress hormone cortisol. And yet we still do it compulsively.

Says writer Tom Stafford in an article for the blog *Mindhacks*, "I must hit the 'get mail' button at least a hundred times a day. Sometimes, if I don't have any new mail, I hit it again immediately, just to check. I interrupt my work to check my mail even when I know that I'm not going to find anything interesting and that I should just concentrate on what I am supposed to be doing."

Compulsively checking your inbox is a habit that supports American psychologist and behaviorist B.F. Skinner's theory of variable rewards. Sometimes the email-checking habit produces a reward, and sometimes it doesn't.

Since you never know which time you check will produce the reward, checking it all the time is reinforced, even when it is pointless and counterproductive.

Breaking this bad habit and becoming more mindful about how you approach your email inbox will not only make you more productive and focused but will also allow you to be more conscious and less reactive to the variable rewards of email.

Action Plan: Begin by being honest with yourself about how many times a day you check your email. If you haven't paid attention to it before, start noticing it now.

Most of those check-ins are pointless and do nothing to increase your productivity, inner peace, or connection to the present moment.

Next, make a conscious decision about how many times a day you need to check email. Would the world fall apart if you only checked it once a day? Maybe your work requires that you check it more often, but try to be honest with yourself about it. A good middle ground is checking three times a day—in the late morning, afternoon, and evening, which is a practice that Steve follows.

Turn off all notifications that pop up or buzz when an email comes in so you can lessen any temptations to check it. Remove any push notifications from your phone. Keep your email tab closed when you are working on your computer so you're not tempted to flip back and forth.

Set aside ten minutes during your email check-in times to review and reply to emails. Any email that requires two minutes or less of your time can be handled right then and there. Any that require more time can be put in an "action folder" to handle later.

Remember that we tend to be less mindful with emails than we are with face-to-face communication. When you receive an email, try to visualize the human face behind the words, as it's easy to misread a person's intentions with email.

When you send an email, be mindful of your language and tone, and remember you're communicating with another human being. Take three deep breaths before hitting the "send" button and ask yourself: "Is it true? Is it necessary? Is it kind?"

Set aside one email check-in time to unsubscribe from the unnecessary junk you receive. You can also get organized by using unroll. me and SaneBox, two resources to help unsubscribe you from lists quickly and group your emails together for better organization.

If you have a hard time breaking the email habit, view your email check-ins as a reward for your focused work or other mindfulness activities. For example, you can only check your email once you complete a project or accomplish a certain number of tasks.

Learn More: Read Steve and Barrie's book *10-Minute Digital Declutter* to help you organize and declutter all of your digital devices and learn how to reduce your dependence on them.

#31. Batch Your Tasks

Did you know that your mind prefers to organize by clumping small, related things into cohesive wholes?

Batching similar tasks, like doing all your writing in one sitting or handling all housekeeping tasks together, makes you more productive and focused.

Grouping tasks also forces you to work longer so that you can enter a "flow state," in which your work becomes easier and more mindful.

When you shift from writing a proposal to checking email then to responding to your coworker's question, for example, your brain gets scrambled. Batching tasks protects us against our self-inflicted distractions—like checking email constantly.

Every time you have to pick up where you left off with a task, you lose time figuring out where you left off and then getting back on track. By the end of the day, you could *lose hours* of focused time because your task planning isn't efficient.

Instead, grouping similar tasks that require similar resources will help streamline their completion and decrease stress and procrastination.

According to author, blogger, and speaker Michael Hyatt, "Batching is setting aside an intentional amount of time for intentional tasks and making an intentional effort to not allow the distractions or interjections of others break that focus."

Action Plan: Before you begin jumping on projects at work (or at home), sit down with pen and paper for ten minutes to create a batching plan.

Here's a simple six-step process to do this:

1. Write a master list of every project and task you need to complete for the day or week.

2. Create batching categories, such as "Making Phone Calls," "Responding to Emails," "Writing Content," "Planning," "Reading," "Researching."

3. Go through your master list, and begin assigning tasks to each category. You may have a few lonesome tasks and some groups that are very large.

4. Tackle the large categories during your most productive time of day, usually in the morning, and use the lonesome tasks as fillers between the larger categories.

5. Schedule easier tasks, like checking email or admin activities for your low-energy times.

6. Try to develop a regular routine around your grouped tasks, performing them at the same time every day. This allows your brain to switch more easily from one batch to the next because it knows what to expect.

The ten-minute habit of batching your tasks is an activity that supports all of your mindfulness efforts. It allows you to focus more intently on your projects, with fewer interruptions and distractions. And it makes you more productive, giving you extra time to spend where you choose to spend it.

Learn More: One of the best resources for learning how to batch tasks and increase your productivity is *Getting Things Done* by David Allen.

#32. Practice the Pomodoro Technique

The Pomodoro Technique is a time-management system developed by Francesco Cirillo in the late 1980s. It's named after the Italian word for tomato, as Cirillo used a kitchen timer shaped like a tomato as his personal timer.

It breaks down work periods into 25-minute intervals (called Pomodoros) with a break between each interval.

The idea behind this technique is to increase productivity. You improve mental agility (and efficiency) by focusing intensely on a task for a short period of time. You then recharge your batteries by taking a quick break.

Even though this intense focus seems difficult, focus in any endeavor is definitely a mindfulness technique. It allows you to immerse yourself in your work with enough engagement that you get into the flow state we referenced earlier.

For those who have difficulty focusing, the Pomodoro Technique definitely helps you maintain presence with your work without tiring quickly or giving into distractions.

Action Plan:

The Pomodoro Technique works in five basic steps:

1. Decide on the task to be done.
2. Set a timer to twenty-five minutes.
3. Work on the task until the timer rings. Record the Pomodoro in writing as a completed task.
4. Take a short break (5 minutes).
5. Work through four Pomodoros and take a longer break (15–20 minutes).

The method emphasizes the importance of task improvement, as well as mindful and focused work. During a Pomodoro session, you're planning, tracking, recording, processing, and visualizing.

Each day, if you prioritize your list of tasks, you can work through these activities in short twenty-five minute intervals.

Learn More: Check out Cirillo's website for more information on using the Pomodoro Technique.

#33. Decrease Distractions

Distraction is the enemy of mindfulness. It's impossible to be present when you are multitasking or mentally pulled in different directions.

Unfortunately, we are constantly faced with distractions, from morning until bedtime. Unless you live in a cave, you will encounter them. They are insidious and oh so alluring, even when we know they compromise our focus and productivity.

Distractions come from your digital devices, the media, other people, and even your own free-floating thoughts that pull you away from the task at hand. Each distraction enters our mind with one mission: harnessing control of our attention and resources.

Says Joe Kraus, founder of Excite and JotSpot, "We are creating and encouraging a culture of distraction where we are increasingly disconnected from the people and events around us, and increasingly unable to engage in long-form thinking. People now feel anxious when their brains are unstimulated."

The irony is that we feel anxiety when we're overstimulated, as well as when we are forced to detach from our stimulating distractions.

We are so addicted to the immediate gratification of giving into distractions that our ability to concentrate for more than a few minutes at a time has atrophied.

The solution is to become conscious of how mindfulness serves your goals and then to manage these distractions accordingly. You must push aside the fear of "missing out" and suffer with a bit of anxiety during times when your mindful attention is required or valuable.

Action Plan: When it's time to engage in some long-form thinking and remain present with a person or task for more than a few minutes, then you need to develop a habit of diminishing distractions.

Here are seven steps to incorporate into your distraction destruction habit:

1. **Turn off your smart phone.** Your phone is likely one of the greatest sources of distraction in your life. The average person checks their phone about 150 times every day (just short of every six waking minutes). If you must keep the phone on, put it on silent and turn off notifications.

2. **Close tabs on your computer.** Close everything except what you are working on. Turn off all notifications from email, social media, etc.

3. **Remove other digital clutter.** Desktop icons, open programs, and other visible files jockey for your mental attention. Look for the digital triggers that distract you, and ruthlessly remove them.

4. **Remove physical clutter.** This is a great time to clear your desk. Anything that is in your field of vision that can distract you (even subconsciously) should be put out of sight.

5. **Give notice to others.** Close your door, and put a "Do Not Disturb" sign on the door. Let the people around you know that you need to be left alone until they see your door open again.

6. **Find your cave.** If you work from home with kids around or in an office with a loud open floor plan, then find another place to work that is quiet and free of distractions. When Barrie was in college and needed to really focus, she would go to a "study closet," which was nothing more than a small closet with a desk.

7. **Take care of your physical needs.** Have your water, tea, or coffee and any food you might want ready on your desk. Make sure the room temperature is to your liking, and use the restroom before you get started.

Learn More: If you want learn more about how to tackle digital distractions head on, read *Sorry, I Have To Take This* by David Rusk and Bradley Kramer. Also check out *Focus: The Hidden Driver of Excellence* by psychologist and journalist Daniel Goleman, who reveals how to sharpen focus even in an era of unstoppable distractions.

#34. Practice Outcome-Directed Thinking

Often we delve into our work with a "Just get it done" mind-set. We plow through the tasks mindlessly, just so we can check the item off the to-do list and move on.

This is especially true with boring or otherwise undesirable endeavors. We push ourselves to begin and complete the work without ever considering why we are performing it or what the outcome will be.

Rather than beginning a task in this state of numbed-out unconsciousness, take a few minutes to think about what you'd like to accomplish by practicing what's called "outcome-directed thinking."

When you focus your attention on a desired outcome rather than on perceived problems, you'll see opportunities where others don't and get through obstacles that may impede other people.

Action Plan: Prior to working on any task, take a few minutes to ask yourself the following questions:

- » Why am I working on this goal, task, or project?
- » What is the obvious outcome of this endeavor?
- » What is the outcome I want to achieve? (Articulate your answer in the most specific terms possible, using positive words related to what you want rather than what you wish to avoid.)
- » What actions do I need to take to ensure I reach my desired outcome? (List these out, as they may be different from your automatic or usual way of approaching this goal or task.)
- » Once I reach this outcome, what will it do for me? (This higher-level question can really boost your motivation and focus as you work toward the outcome.)

You can reinforce your outcome-directed thinking habit by practicing affirmations and visualization, as we suggested earlier. Think of the exact outcomes you wish to see with any goal, task, or project.

Keep track of outcomes that you've accomplished after you complete your task to see if it matches your desired outcome articulated before you began the project.

Learn More: You can learn more about outcome-based thinking by reading this article.

#35. Find Your Flow State

In his bestselling book *Flow: The Psychology of Optimal Experience*, Hungarian psychologist Mihaly Csikszentmihalyi (pronounced Me-high Cheek-sent-me-high) defines flow as "a state in which people are so involved in an activity that nothing else seems to matter; the experience is so enjoyable that people will continue to do it even at great cost, for the sheer sake of doing it."

During a flow state, a person is completely absorbed in a task or project, especially one that involves creative abilities. As they engage in the activity, they feel "strong, alert, in effortless control, unselfconscious, and at the peak of their abilities."

As we mentioned earlier, flow is the ultimate form mindfulness in action. You are completely engaged to the extent that all distractions fall away, and you are one with the task at hand.

This is the state of mind you want to achieve with any focused effort you perform at work or in your personal life.

According to Dr. Csikszentmihalyi, the flow state includes seven key components:

1. You're completely involved in what you're doing with focus and concentration.
2. There's a sense of ecstasy during which you're outside of everyday reality.
3. There's a great inner clarity where you know what needs to be done, and you receive immediate feedback on how well you're doing.
4. You know that the activity is doable and that you have the

necessary skills to complete it successfully.

5. You lose your sense of self, and all of your worries and concerns drift away.

6. You lose track of time, and you're completely focused on the present moment.

7. There's an intrinsic motivation—whatever produces flow becomes its own reward.

Action Plan: You can achieve flow state by doing the following six actions:

1. **Find a challenge.** Choose an activity or task that you enjoy doing and find somewhat challenging.

2. **Develop your skills.** In order to be able to meet the challenge, you have to develop your skills and become proficient. If the activity is too easy, you'll quickly grow bored.

3. **Set clear goals.** You need to be very clear on what you want to achieve with your activity and how you'll know if you're succeeding.

4. **Focus on the task at hand.** Eliminate all other distractions. You don't want anything to pull your attention away from the task or disrupt the state you're in.

5. **Set aside enough time.** It will take you about ten minutes to get into the flow state and a while longer after that until you feel fully present and immersed in the activity.

6. **Monitor your emotional state.** If you're having trouble entering the flow state, check in with your emotions. If you're in an aroused state of anxiety, try a calming exercise like breathing or meditation.

Learn More: Read the book *Flow: The Psychology of Optimal Experience*, by Mihaly Csikszentmihaly for more skills on practicing flow.

PART V

AFTERNOON MINDFULNESS HABITS

#36. Practice "Slow Work"

A critical part of being present in the moment and finding a state of flow with your work is slowing down with everything you do.

When you rush from one task to the next, trying to cram in as much effort as possible, you lose the sense of accomplishment that comes with the process.

Says author and relationship expert Margaret Paul, PhD, "When your sense of worth is attached to the effort you make and putting forth your very best, then the process itself becomes exciting and rewarding, regardless of the outcome."

In a society that places high value on speed and productivity, slowing down might make you feel like you're not giving your best effort. But taking more time to thoroughly complete each task will ultimately make you more productive and successful.

According to a recent article in *Time* magazine, "the philosophy of 'slow work' challenges the unsustainable practice of doing everything as fast as possible and offers an alternative workplace framework for energizing people and helping people better align their personal and professional priorities. It urges us to punctuate our routines in ways that might initially appear to compromise productivity but actually enhance long-term creativity."

Rather than racing to check everything off your list, make a conscious effort to slow down in all of your endeavors—whether it's washing the dishes or completing a project at work.

Action Plan: Here are five ways you can slow down at work and in your personal life and still be productive:

1. **Give yourself more time for each task.** Rather than attempting to complete a project or task as quickly as possible, double the amount of time you believe it will take to complete the task. This removes a lot of the pressure to complete a task quickly, reducing feelings of stress and anxiety.

2. **Do just one thing at a time.** Multitasking is the enemy of mindfulness. Focus on the task at hand without attempting to work on anything else at the same time.

3. **Learn to say no.** Don't feel obligated to interrupt your work whenever someone needs your attention. Prioritize the project or task you are working on over the needs of other people and their requests.

4. **Focus on excellence.** Rather than focusing on speed, shift your focus to excellence. Spend your time doing the best job possible in every endeavor, and you will feel much greater satisfaction with your work.

5. **Enjoy the process.** Most of your time is spent in the process rather than celebrating an outcome. It is satisfying to reach an outcome, especially if it's a positive outcome. However, if we wait for outcomes before we experience joy, we rob ourselves of happiness and satisfaction. The real joy is in the doing rather than achieving the final result.

Learn More: If you're interested in learning more benefits from slowing down in work and your personal life, read the book *In Praise of Slowness: Challenging the Cult of Speed* by Carl Honore.

#37. Be Present with Peers

Busyness, stress, and distractions not only compromise your satisfaction with your work, but they also undermine your relationships with coworkers and peers.

One of the common complaints people have about their jobs involves their interactions with a boss, client, or peer. The pressure to perform coupled with personality differences creates an environment ripe for conflict and competition.

Civility, kindness, and compassion are often viewed as being incompatible with many work environments where "the bottom line" supersedes healthy communication.

Some organizations are discovering the importance of cultivating emotional intelligence in the workplace, recognizing that those with empathy, self-awareness, people skills, and self-regulation are essential to the health of the business.

You can contribute to a more emotionally intelligent work environment, as well as your own peace of mind, by being more present with the people you work with. Just a few minutes a day of being more present can make a huge difference in your satisfaction at work.

Action Plan: Being present with others simply means paying more attention in a spirit of care and compassion, without allowing distractions to pull you away. Here are five steps you can use to get the most out of every interaction:

1. **Look people in the eye.** Simply looking at someone when speaking or listening will make the other person feel a connection to you. They will know they have your full attention.

2. **Practice empathic listening.** Remain completely attentive to what the other person is saying. Don't allow distractions to pull you away. Avoid interrupting the other person, even when you have something important to say.

3. **Speak mindfully.** As we mention in our book *Declutter Your Mind*, "Resist the temptation to simply react to someone's words or actions. Take a moment to choose your words carefully. Speak in ways that are loving, compassionate, and respectful, and try to use a calm, non-threatening voice, even if the other person is agitated or angry."

4. **Be more caring.** Treat the people around you with loving-kindness, even if they are angry or rude. Being kind and compassionate is not incompatible with being a good coworker or boss.

5. **Reserve judgments.** Pay attention to mental comparisons and evaluations of others when you are speaking with them. Remain open-minded and curious rather than jumping to conclusions about the other person.

Learn More: To learn more about emotional intelligence in the workplace, check out *Emotional Intelligence 2.0* by Travis Bradberry and Jean Greaves.

Also check out this article on eleven ways to be more mindful in your relationships at work.

#38. Cultivate a Beginner's Mind

Says Zen monk, author, and teacher Shunryu Suzuki, "In the beginner's mind there are many possibilities, but in the expert's there are few."

A beginner's mind is a concept in Zen Buddhism known as *shoshin*.

What does it mean to cultivate a beginner's mind? It means you develop a willingness to release preconceived notions about the way things should be based on your existing knowledge or beliefs.

In your work (and in life), having a beginner's mind-set allows you access to a heightened awareness of various options for success in any endeavor. Your mind is open to *all* possibilities.

With a beginner's mind-set, you temporarily suspend all of your opinions, knowledge, and strongly held beliefs so that you can explore an idea without mental limitations.

Even if you are an expert in your profession, remaining open-minded might let you discover potential solutions that you did not know existed previously or that don't match your expertise.

You keep your options open, you respond more mindfully and thoughtfully to the circumstances in the moment, rather than just relying on past experience.

Action Plan: When you approach a new project or task during your day, take a few deep breaths before you begin. Then visualize your mind as a blank slate with all your previous knowledge and experience erased.

Ask yourself the question, "How can I approach this project

differently?" Rather than immediately returning to standard operating procedures, allow your mind the time to brainstorm new options.

If you need to use past experience as a guide, think about how you can apply this experience in a different way.

Let go of common sense for the moment, and step out of your comfort zone to give yourself the freedom to explore even the wildest possibilities. Sometimes these out-of-the-box, unexpected ideas turn out to be the most creative solutions.

As you are practicing a beginner's mind-set, try to let go of the fear of failure. Suspend it for just a few minutes, and assume that success is the only possible outcome.

Pay attention to your instincts and inner creative voice. Don't look over your shoulder at what everyone else is doing. Pull from the wellspring of your own unique perspective and ideas. This is how innovation occurs.

In meetings or group settings, invite group members to leave their expertise at the door. Ask them to approach the problem or challenge with a fresh set of eyes and an open mind. Invite people to join the meeting who are complete novices and can view the situation with untainted innocence.

You can apply the strategies in any situation in which you desire fresh, mindful thinking for a challenge or problem, whether in your personal or professional life.

Learn More: Check out this podcast called "The Beginner's Mind: Why Naiveté Is a Critical Business Asset."

Also read the book *Zen Mind, Beginner's Mind* by Shunryu Suzuki.

#39. Create Mindful Meetings

Do you work in an environment where you must regularly partici-pate in meetings?

If so, then you probably know that meetings can be a big drain on your energy and productivity. They are often not even relevant to your most pressing work priorities or long-term goals.

As economist John Kenneth Galbraith once said, "Meetings are indispensable when you don't want to do anything." According to a 3M Meeting Network survey of executives, 25 to 50% of the time people spend in meetings is wasted.

Even so, some meetings are required for your position or volunteer activities. You may be responsible for leading meetings yourself, in addition to participating in meetings called by others.

Meetings can be a great time to reconnect with your peers and to practice a beginner's mind-set as you address challenges, generate ideas, and look for solutions.

Rather than thinking of meetings as a waste of time, you can practice mindfulness before and during meetings to make them more valuable to you and other attendees.

Action Plan: Here is a list of five strategies you can use to get the most from each meeting that you attend.

1. **Tune into your emotions before the meeting.** Are you feeling anxious? Angry? Overwhelmed? Take a few minutes

to monitor your emotions and recalibrate them so you enter the meeting with a positive mind-set.

2. **Encourage a beginner's mind-set.** At the beginning of a meeting, let the members know that all ideas and questions are invited. Encourage out-of-the-box thinking.

3. **Request mutual respect and acceptance.** Let group members know that this meeting is a safe space where members will not be judged or put down for their input or ideas.

4. **Offer positive feedback.** When a group member speaks, reflect back to them what you heard them say and provide positive and encouraging feedback.

5. **Remain focused.** If you were leading the meeting, be conscientious about keeping the meeting brief and to the point. Stay focused on the topic of the meeting and the agenda you have prepared.

Learn More: Interested in creating more productive, mindful meetings? Check out the books *Meetings Suck: Turning One of the Most Loathed Elements of Business into One of the Most Valuable* by Cameron Herold and *Meetings Matter: 8 Powerful Strategies for Remarkable Conversations* by Paul Axtell.

#40. Stand, Stretch, and Get Moving

Steve and Barrie spend most of their workdays sitting in front of a computer. Maybe you do as well. Whether you work from home or in an office, working at a desk all day can cause you to tune out to the needs of your body.

In fact, research links sitting for long periods (whether at work, in front of the TV, or in your car) with obesity, cardiovascular disease, and cancer.

Even if you spend time every week at the gym or exercising, it doesn't offset the negative impact of extended sitting.

Studies show that your body can benefit from simply standing up, stretching your muscles, and moving around for a few minutes. Think of standing and stretching as pushing the reset button on your body.

When you are mindful of all the ways your body serves you, you'll be more inclined to treat it respectfully, even in the midst of a busy workday.

Action Plan: Says Gretchen Reynolds in her book *The First 20 Minutes: Surprising Science Reveals How We Can Exercise Better, Train Smarter, Live Longer*:

> New science shows very persuasively that standing up about every 20 minutes, even for only a minute or two, reduces your risks of developing diabetes and heart disease.

> By standing up, you cause the big muscles in your legs and back to contract, which leads to an increase in certain enzymes that break up fat in the blood stream. You don't have to jog in place or do jumping jacks. Just stand. A very pleasant additional benefit is that standing up every 20 to 30 minutes also seems to prompt the body to burn calories, so you don't gain as much weight from sitting at the office most of the day.

Since twenty minutes appears to be the magic number, set your phone timer, FitBit, or clock alarm to ring or vibrate every twenty minutes during your sedentary times of day.

Although just standing up is enough to reduce your risks of certain diseases, we suggest you use this standing time to become more mindful about your body.

As you are standing, close your eyes and pay attention to any areas of your body where you feel tension, pain, or stress. Breathe deeply into these tense areas, stretching them slowly as you exhale.

Then raise your arms over your head and reach for the ceiling. Bend backward as far as is comfortable, stretching your neck and back.

Keeping your arms raised, bend at the waist and slowly drop your arms, head, and torso toward the floor for a full-body stretch. Try to touch the floor if possible. As you are bent over, take one more deep breath, and on the exhale, relax your body into the stretch as you reach to the floor.

Stand up and hold your right arm in the air by your head. Stretch to the left, bending at the waist as far as you can. Do this on the left side as well.

Bend your head slowly to the right and left, and then move it in a circle, going left and right.

Take a few more deep, cleansing breaths with your eyes closed before you sit back down.

Learn More: Check out Gretchen Reynolds's book *The First 20 Minutes: Surprising Science Reveals How We Can Exercise Better, Train Smarter, Live Longer.* You might also benefit from the exercises in *Mindful Movements: Ten Exercises for Well-Being* by Thích Nhất Hạnh.

#41. Take a Digital Break

You might get hundreds of emails every day. Social media and news updates are popping up left and right, and your smart phone is constantly buzzing with calls, texts, and notifications. Before you even have a chance to begin your workday in earnest, your head is already spinning with messages, demands, and extraneous information.

Although our digital devices can make us more productive, they can also deplete our energy and creativity, especially when we begin the week with digital distractions. Our attachment to our devices keeps us in a state of low-level anxiety.

When we feel overwhelmed at work, our first instinct is to turn to our devices as a source of comfort. We compulsively check emails and waste time on social media to feel engaged and relevant.

Sadly, our digital devices often don't provide the peace of mind that we are seeking. Instead, they further distract us both from our work and our ability to be present.

This excessive connectivity also creates a false sense of urgency, as though we are missing something important if we are not constantly plugged in.

Says coach and writer Kate Swoboda in an article for the blog Tiny Buddha, "Taking a digital break is about being willing to surrender, to let go completely, and to trust that when you return, it's all going to be okay."

In fact, mindfully stepping away from your digital devices for short periods of time during your day allows you to feel more focused and centered when you do plug back in.

Action Plan: Try to take two or three mini-digital breaks during your workday for about ten minutes each. Start with just one if that's all you feel comfortable doing.

Close down your computer and turn off your phone. Set a timer for ten minutes. And use this time to break mindfully in a way that contributes to a calm but engaged state of mind.

Consider one of the following activities during this digital break:

- » Meditate for ten minutes.
- » Go outside and take a walk.
- » Do your stand-and-stretch exercises.
- » Outline a project or write down your goals in longhand.
- » Have a conversation with a coworker.
- » Mindfully make a cup of tea and drink it.
- » Do some inspirational reading.
- » Clear some clutter in your workspace.
- » Brainstorm or create a mind map.

When the timer goes off, you can return to your devices with a clear head and a more focused state of mind.

Learn More: If you'd like to learn more about unplugging from your digital devices, check out the book *Digital Detox: Unplug To Reclaim Your Life* by Damon Zahariades.

#42. Tune into Your Moods

At the beginning of this book, we shared a scenario about a person whose day began with stress, distraction, and overwhelm. By the time he made it to work, he was already in a bad mood, brimming with agitation.

Just consider how starting your day in a negative state can have a negative impact on your work performance, not to mention your job satisfaction. In fact, research shows that bad moods lead to procrastination, while feelings of happiness increase both productivity and success.

Most people are so busy and distracted at work or during their daily activities that they don't pay attention to their emotions.

They may notice stress, physical symptoms, or frustration, but they aren't tuned in enough to consciously acknowledge their feelings or notice how their moods are impacting the quality of their work.

Even when we are aware of our shifting moods, we often don't take the time to improve our moods to be more productive and positive. Maybe we don't even know that it's possible to impact our own mental state.

By taking just a few minutes to tune into your moods, evaluate your feelings, and work to change them, you can upgrade the quality of your work.

Action Plan: Shut your door, power down your computer, and turn off your phone. Close your eyes, and take a few deep, cleansing breaths.

Perform a mental scan of your body, paying attention to any feelings of muscle tension, tightness in your chest, headache, or shortness of breath. These physical feelings are good indicators of a negative emotional state.

Ask yourself the question, "What is my mood right now?" Sit quietly for a few minutes and pay attention to your mental and emotional state. Try to isolate exactly the emotions you are feeling.

Once you identify your mood (overwhelmed, frustrated, sad, angry, etc.), then ask yourself, "What are the thoughts behind these feelings?" For example, you might say, "I feel angry because my boss disrespected me in the meeting."

Also ask yourself, "What was I doing right before I began to feel this way? What thought or conclusion did I come to that contributed to this negative mood?"

If you can identify the "thinking trap" that contributed to your bad mood, you can create a positive mental state.

In the example above, the trap might be, "My boss must really think I'm a loser. He hates me." To fix this, you could ask yourself, "Are my thoughts about this situation really true or the entire truth? What is a more positive or productive way of thinking about this situation? Does my boss *actually* hate me?"

Replace your original negative thoughts with something more accurate and rational, and you will notice that your mood shifts in a more positive direction. For example, you might say, "My boss wasn't respectful in the meeting, but he has treated me respectfully many times in the past and has praised my work."

By using more realistic and positive language, you'll feel relief from the tension and frustration of "all or nothing" thinking. With practice, you'll develop the habit of tuning into your moods and changing your thoughts accordingly.

Learn More: If you have trouble identifying your moods, check out this list of common moods and mood descriptions. You can learn more about managing your moods by reading the book *Mind Over Mood* by Dennis Greenberger, PhD, and Christine A. Padesky, PhD.

#43. Show Appreciation

One of the simplest but most effective mindfulness habits to build is showing appreciation to the people around you.

William James, well-known psychologist and philosopher, said, "The deepest principle of human nature is a craving to be appreciated." Everyone wants to feel valued and recognized for their contributions and accomplishments.

In our busy and distracted lives, it's easy to neglect showing appreciation to the people we work or interact with on a daily basis. We are so consumed with our own thoughts, tasks, and obligations that we are unconscious of the many ways others support and help us.

Taking others for granted in our personal and professional lives is a certain way to undermine the quality of our relationships and push people away from us.

When you express your gratitude and appreciation to someone, you not only enhance their lives, but you enrich your own as well, as you can see the immediate impact your kind words have on the other person.

Taking the time to express appreciation shows that you are fully present with the other person and tuned into their essential worthiness and their humanity.

Appreciation creates a moment that will forever be embedded in the mind of the recipient, which enhances your connection with this person.

When you take the simple action of expressing appreciation, others will be drawn to you like a magnet, and their respect for you will grow.

Action Plan: Take a few minutes to think about the people you've encountered during the day or week who you appreciate. Write down the name of each person and what they said or did that you want to acknowledge. Make a note about how each person's actions positively impacted you, and reflect on that for a moment. These individuals can be friends, family members, coworkers, or random strangers you've encountered throughout the day.

Think about how you want to show your appreciation to each of these people. Do you want to speak with them in person? Make a phone call? Or send an email or letter? Take a few minutes to communicate your appreciation to each of these people.

Be very specific and genuine in your praise for the person's actions, without any expectation of praise in return. When you acknowledge someone in person, try to use his or her name and make eye contact as you are speaking.

Throughout the day, remain mindful of showing appreciation to those you encounter who do something nice for you or provide service to you. Train yourself to view others through the eyes of appreciation for who they are and what they offer the world.

Learn More: If you'd like to learn more about showing appreciation in the workplace, read the book *The 5 Languages of Appreciation in the Workplace: Empowering Organizations by Encouraging People* by Gary Chapman and Paul E. White.

You might also enjoy *Focus on the Good Stuff: The Power of Appreciation* by Mike Robbins and Richard Carlson.

Finally, you could check out Mike Robbins's TED Talk on the power of appreciation.

#44. Practice Strategic Acceptance

Often in our daily lives, things just don't go according to our expectations. People let us down. We encounter a challenging setback. We are surprised by an unpleasant or negative outcome.

Our first reaction when things don't go our way is to push back and try to set things back on course. We try to fix it. That's a productive reaction if change is possible, but many times a setback simply is what it is. There's nothing you can do to change the outcome or make things better.

So our next reaction is to fall into the catastrophic thinking loop, believing the setback or disappointment is far worse than it really is. These out-of-proportion thoughts can produce anger, frustration, sadness, and anxiety—moods that further hamper our peace of mind.

By practicing strategic acceptance, both about the negative situation and your reaction to it, you can find peace in moving forward in spite of the unexpected event.

As you take a few mindful moments to acknowledge your feelings, you clear the way for finding solutions, moving in a new direction, or simply letting go.

Action Plan: When you encounter an unexpected negative event or disappointment during your day, try to step away from other people to be alone for a few minutes.

To help you calm down, focus on your breathing. Sit down, close your eyes, and breathe to a count of ten several times until you are less agitated.

Next, tune into your emotions, as explained in Habit #42. Identify the emotion(s) you feel in the moment related to this setback. Is it anger? Fear? Disappointment? Jealousy?

Rather than trying to change the emotion right now, simply accept how you are feeling about the situation.

You might say to yourself, "I feel so angry at Susan for missing the deadline and making us lose the contract."

Acknowledging and accepting your emotions about the situation will release some of your stress so that you have the mental bandwidth to take appropriate next steps.

Ask yourself if there's anything you can do to change or improve the situation. If so, make a list of action steps you can take when you are in a better frame of mind.

If there is nothing you can do right now to salvage or improve the situation, then acknowledge that to yourself and sit with it for a few minutes. You might say to yourself something like, "We have lost that contract. There's nothing I can do to change that. I now accept that."

Close your eyes and visualize putting the setback inside a helium balloon. Then see yourself releasing the balloon, and watch it float away and disappear out of sight. Say to yourself, "I release this situation. I am willing to let it go." Take another few deep and cleansing breaths before returning to your day.

Depending on the difficulty or impact of the negative situation, you may need to go through these steps several times in order to process your feelings and move past the event.

#45. Be an Objective Advisor

Whether at work, in your relationships, or with daily life in general, you often encounter challenges that are complicated, confusing, and emotionally charged.

When you're caught up in the details of the issue, it's hard to have the clarity to untangle the problem or to take the best next steps. Every choice feels fraught with potential negative consequences, and your emotions may be so overwhelming that you can't think clearly.

Getting outside feedback and advice can be helpful, but the best place to begin looking for solutions is within yourself. You need to be your own coach or advisor, tapping into your inner wisdom and intuition to lead you to the best course of action.

A simple mindfulness technique can help you move forward and connect with your inner wisdom. Remember earlier when we discussed being the observer of your thoughts, as though a separate "you" is watching your thoughts in your mind?

Now we want you to find that separate part of yourself again, but this time as the "objective advisor" who can draw from your conscious and subconscious awareness to help you reach a sound conclusion or find a solution.

Action Plan: Have paper and pen handy to use throughout this exercise. Take a few deep, cleansing breaths to clear your head until you feel relaxed.

Get started, by writing down the challenge you're facing in specific terms. For example, you might write, "I don't know whether I should take this new job opportunity or stay in my current job."

Next, close your eyes and visualize yourself sitting in a chair with another chair directly across from you. Now see another you, the "objective advisor" you, sitting down in that chair, ready to assist you.

Ask your objective advisor a question about your challenge—something like, "What do I need to know about this situation?" Start with an open-ended question like this, rather than a yes or no question.

Sit quietly for a few minutes and wait for a response to arise in your mind. Or you may visualize your objective self providing a response.

You can ask additional questions like, "What is the best course of action?" or "How can I deal with the consequences of this decision?" or "What do I need to do right now?" Ask yourself as many questions as you wish in order to fully explore your cognitive resources.

Write down any answers that come up for you, and consider them logically to ensure they aren't just immediate emotional reactions to the situation.

If you don't get an answer, or if your thoughts are too jumbled to get a clear response, wait until later when you are calmer, and try the exercise again.

Use the insights you receive from this exercise to help you move forward with your decision. But use them in combination with other valid resources, such as feedback from trusted advisors or conducting research around the problem.

The more insights and information you have at your disposal, the more confident you'll feel in your actions or decisions.

Learn More: You might be interested in the blog post by Barrie called, "How to Make a Big Decision without Regret." Also watch this TED Talk on intuitive decision making.

#46. Brainstorm with Mind Maps

If you're in a profession that requires thinking creatively and generating new ideas, or if you want to figure out creative solutions in your personal life, mind mapping is an excellent mindfulness tool.

A mind map is a diagram that connects ideas and information around a central topic or problem. It is like a tree with many extending branches. In the center is the main idea, and the branches are the subtopics that you brainstorm related to this central topic.

Using a mind map, rather than a more linear note-taking process, supports your mindfulness efforts in many ways. Because you use words, images, numbers, and color, a mind map is six times better in helping you retain information than by words alone.

According to author Tony Buzan, who popularized mind mapping, the exercise allows you to perform whole brain processing by using the entire range of your cortical skills. A mind map reflects how our brains process and recall information, in a dynamic manner where you can expand on each idea and strategy.

Mind mapping also encourages linking or grouping concepts through natural associations that arise during the mapping process. This helps you come up with more ideas and find deeper meanings related to your topic.

You will become deeply engaged in the mind mapping process, entering the "flow state," as your brain makes natural associations, bouncing one idea off another, during the process of thinking, writing, and drawing.

Action Plan: Find a quiet space, free of distractions and interruptions. Use a short meditation or breathing exercise to get in a good mental space for your mind mapping exercise.

Grab a sheet of paper and pen (or several pens in different colors). You can also use colored pencils. Mind mapping by hand (rather than using your computer) provides more cognitive stimulation and focused engagement.

Begin by simply brainstorming your topic, free associating ideas and thoughts that come to mind as you consider the subject. You don't need to organize these thoughts—just let them spill out and write them down.

In the center of the page, draw a box or a circle, and draw an image or picture of your main idea, topic, or problem. Drawing an image is important as your brain responds more to visual stimuli. Also, use a keyword to identify the topic.

Next, add branches to the main idea using a different color for each branch. These first branches represent the main subtopics of your central theme. Use keywords to explain these subtopics.

Mentally explore each of these subtopics to build smaller branches on the mind map, maintaining the same colors for the smaller branches that you used for the sub-branches, so you can visually follow a pattern of ideas through color-coding. Add your keywords or phrases here as well.

Go back through your mind map and include some images or symbols that reflect your themes and keywords. You don't have to be a trained artist to draw these images. Just allow your creativity to flow through drawing, as images are visual stimuli that will help you recall and process information.

You want to create an "image-rich network," which Buzan suggests is the essence of a mind map. You can use lines, symbols, arrows, boxes, etc. to bring your map to life.

Continue to branch out with your mind map as you come up with additional ideas and inspiration. You might need to go back to some of your subcategories to add more branches as creative ideas start to flow.

Try to avoid judging your mind map (or your artistic ability) as you work on it, or even once it's completed. View *the process* of creating this map as an enjoyable mindfulness habit that sparks your creativity and unleashes a wellspring of ideas and insights you may not have been able to tap otherwise.

Learn More: You can learn more about the power of mind mapping for creativity and mindfulness in this TED Talk by Tony Buzan, the founder of mind mapping. Also check out Tony's website for more ideas and a variety of videos on creating your own mind map.

You can also create digital mind maps through software programs like iMindMap and MindMeister.

#47. Take a Music Break

Listening to music is a powerful mindfulness habit that can reduce stress, elevate your mood, raise your IQ, and offer many other mental and physical health benefits.

Taking a break to actively listen to music for a few minutes during your day can help you return to your work in a more positive, peaceful, and productive frame of mind. In fact, listening to music— especially classical music—can change your brain in ways that improve memory and learning.

Enjoying and appreciating music can be more than a simply aesthetic pleasure or a pleasant background noise for whatever else we happen to be doing. Actively listening to music is a portal to our inner worlds, allowing us to better understand our thoughts and emotions.

Music is a powerful art form that spans social, political, and language barriers, touching common experiences that are beyond words.

It can be healing, energizing, calming, and enlightening. It opens deep parts of ourselves that we might otherwise not access when we allow ourselves to be fully immersed in the experience of deep listening.

As American composer Michael Torke says, "Why waste money on psychotherapy when you can listen to the [Bach's] B Minor Mass?"

For listening to music to be a mindfulness habit, you must open yourself to it with your whole being. Just like any other mindfulness activity, listening to music mindfully requires your full attention in the present moment.

Action Plan: Find a comfortable place to listen to music without interruptions or distractions. Turn off your phone and computer and anything else that might buzz or ding.

If other people are nearby who might be disturbed by your music, be sure to use headphones.

Decide on the type of music that best suits your mood or your goals for the day. If you are looking to relax and calm down, you might choose light jazz or classical, for example. If you want to improve your mood, you could choose some "feel good" songs.

Take a few moments to consider all that went into creating the music—the instrument makers, the composer, the training time for the artists, etc. Try to be mindful of everything involved in the one piece of music you are about to enjoy. Notice the various instruments used, the rhythm, the melody, and the vocal arrangements (if there are any). Let your mind rest in the sensation of these intense sounds.

Turn your attention next to how the music makes you feel. What emotions are arising as you listen? Do you feel a sense of calm? Are you energized? Do you notice the music brings up old memories or feelings? Observe your emotions without judgment. Just notice them.

Visualize yourself as part of the music. You are riding the waves of sound and rhythm and becoming integrated with them.

If your attention wanders during the song, gently guide your attention back to the music.

Once the song ends, take a few moments to reflect on what you just heard. Sit with your feelings and the memory of the music. Take a few deep breaths and open your eyes.

Learn More: If you want to listen to music for relaxation, you can find ten pieces of music designed to help you relax in this article. Also check out *Mozart for Meditation—Quiet Music for Quiet Times,* which you can find on Amazon in a CD, MP3, or cassette.

#48. Cultivate Humility

Humility is a much underrated and misunderstood quality. Certainly in Western culture, and particularly in today's political climate, humility might be viewed as weakness or insecurity.

We are conditioned with a competitive reflex that compels us to outdo or oppose others who make us feel threatened in some way.

Humility is a subtle concept that is worth cultivating as a gateway to mindfulness. The word "humility" comes from the Latin word *humilis*, which means "grounded." When you are humble, you are grounded in yourself with enough self-assurance and poise that you don't need to show off, act defensive, or toot your own horn.

When you practice humility, you intentionally let go of self-aggrandizing behaviors and thoughts that put you in a "me first" frame of mind. Working toward humility is a growth experience in which you no longer need to see yourself above others—nor do you put yourself below them.

You have a sense of confident neutrality about who you are as compared to others. You view your own strengths and weaknesses accurately, and you recognize that everyone has intrinsic value, even those who appear "beneath" you in some way.

Many spiritual traditions, like Buddhism, view the cultivation of humility as a necessary step on the path toward enlightenment. If fact, humility, gratitude, and mindfulness are intrinsically intertwined.

When you focus on gratitude for others, you are purposefully mindful of how people in various walks of life have helped you. Through gratitude and awareness of your inner dependence on others, you become more humble.

Cultivating humility has the added benefit of making you more attractive and approachable. A report published in *The Journal of Positive Psychology* revealed that people found dating partners with higher humility more attractive than those with low humility scores.

You've probably noticed that those in your work or personal life who are in leadership positions and who practice humility are generally well liked and respected. The greatest leaders don't look to blame others to protect themselves or try to steal the spotlight. Through humility and a spirit of generosity, they inspire and motivate those around them.

Practicing humility is something you can focus on as a daily mindfulness habit, but it must also be applied in your daily interactions with others.

Action Plan: Find a quiet space where you won't be distracted or interrupted. Turn off or silence all of your digital devices. Sitting in a chair, take a few deep, calming breaths before you begin this practice.

Once your mind is calm and quiet, take a few minutes to think about your strengths and weaknesses. Think about these traits the way a loving friend would describe you—with honesty and clarity, unfiltered by ego or defensiveness.

Next, think about the people who have helped you develop your strengths and those who have supported you in areas where you aren't as strong or accomplished. Focus on your gratitude for those people who have impacted your life in these ways.

Take a few minutes to review your day, and silently acknowledge all of the people who have made your life easier or helped you in some way today. This could be anyone from the barista at Starbucks who made your coffee to your coworker who helped you finish a project.

Finally, take a minute to notice any feelings of judgment, defensiveness, insecurity, or pride you might be holding on to. How can humility help you resolve these feelings? Visualize your negative feelings dissolving as you infuse them with humility. Acknowledge that you don't always know best, that your way isn't the only way, that you are no better or worse than anyone.

End this session with a few more deep breaths before you return to your day. Use the mindful energy of humility that you developed during your ten-minute session and apply it with others throughout your day. Show appreciation, acknowledge others, offer assistance, build someone up, reserve judgments.

Learn More: If you'd like to be inspired by stories of people from all walks of life who have demonstrated humility, check out the book *Humility: The Secret Ingredient of Success* by Pat Williams and Jim Denney.

Also check out the timely book *Humility Is the New Smart: Rethinking Human Excellence in the Smart Machine Age* by Edward D. Hess and Katherine Ludwig.

And if you are interested in humility as a spiritual practice, check out *The Science and Practice of Humility: The Path to Ultimate Freedom* by Jason Gregory.

#49. Practice a Growth Mind-set

Dr. Carol Dweck, Professor of Psychology at Stanford University and one of the world's leading researchers in the field of motivation, has spent decades researching achievement and success, and through her research she's discovered something groundbreaking—the power of our mind-set.

She has learned that talent and skills aren't the only elements of success. A major factor is whether we have what she calls a "fixed" mind-set or a "growth" mind-set.

Those with a fixed mind-set believe their intelligence, qualities, and abilities are set in stone, but they have an urgency to prove those qualities over and over. The main goal is to appear smart, capable, and to avoid failure at all costs. When these people do fail, they view it as a direct measure of their competence and self-worth.

With a growth mind-set, you believe change is possible and even necessary. You don't view failures as the end of the world—you see them as opportunities for learning. You are comfortable with taking risks, and you even seek out calculated risk opportunities.

You want to challenge yourself to try something harder, stretch beyond your perceived limitations, and go for things others might not think you're capable of achieving.

Dr. Dweck's research has shown that the growth mind-set creates a love of learning and a resilience that's essential for great accomplishment. A growth mind-set provides motivation and productivity in business, education, personal habits, relationships, and sports.

Says Dweck, "In a growth mindset, people believe that their most basic abilities can be developed through dedication and hard work—brains and talent are just the starting point."

Fortunately, Dr. Dweck has shown that it is possible to change your own mind-set from fixed to growth. Our mind-sets exist on a continuum, and by applying certain strategies, you can move further on the continuum toward growth.

Applying strategies to reinforce a growth mind-set is an exercise in mindfulness. With a growth mind-set, you aren't tangled up in the past or the future (except to the extent you are creating goals and plans). You are giving attention to the present moment by being open to new possibilities and stretching yourself beyond your limiting beliefs with focused attention in the now.

When you step back and pay attention to your mind-set and work to shift it from a fixed to a growth mind-set, you can alter the trajectory of your day. You can improve your peace of mind simply by making the effort to shift your beliefs about yourself and your abilities.

Action Plan: Find a quiet place to think without distraction, and grab a pen and paper to make notes. Begin with a quiet self-assessment of your own mind-set. Close your eyes, take a few deep, cleansing breaths, and ask yourself how you might be reinforcing a fixed mind-set.

Notice how you have reacted to challenges, failures, or opportunities for taking risks in the past. How often do you limit yourself, undermine your potential, or bristle when someone suggests you are wrong? What is your self-talk when you make a mistake or fail at something? Write down your answers.

Think about the triggers that put you back into a fixed mind-set. It's easy to feel insecure when faced with certain challenges. What beliefs or events trigger those reactions from you? Write your answers to these questions as well.

Next, question these fixed mind-set beliefs and attitudes. How can you challenge yourself to try harder, stretch yourself beyond your perceived limitations, and view failure or mistakes in a more positive light? How can you change the way you talk to yourself so you invite opportunity rather than shutting it down? Write down your thoughts about these questions.

An important part of shifting toward a growth mind-set is understanding the science behind the concept. Dr. Dweck found that people's beliefs about their own intelligence had a significant impact on their motivation, effort, and approach to challenges.

According to Dweck's research and years of previous research on neuroplasticity, the brain can grow with learning, and intelligence is malleable.

Spend a few minutes focused on these findings and what they mean for you. Repeat an affirmation to yourself, "I am capable of doing and achieving more than I believe. I embrace challenges. I am persistent. I see effort as the path to mastery. I can learn from criticism and failure."

The key to activating this new habit is applying it in daily life. Knowing that the science of mind-set opens doors of possibility for you, look for ways to stretch yourself and your assumptions. Set high standards and assume that you can meet them, while enjoying the process of working toward your goals.

Learn More: Read Dr. Carol Dweck's book *Mindset: The New Psychology of Success* and see her TED Talk on the power of believing that you can improve.

#50. Notice Your Body Language

Practicing mindful speaking and active listening are highly valuable strategies for improving the quality of your relationships. But effective and mindful communication involves more than your mouth and your ears. It involves your entire body.

What you do with your body and your facial expressions communicates to other people your true feelings and intentions more than words do.

Says social psychologist, author, and lecturer Amy Cuddy, "We make sweeping judgments and inferences from body language. And those judgments can predict really meaningful life outcomes like who we hire or promote, who we ask out on a date."

But our body language doesn't just impact the way others perceive us. It can change the way we feel about ourselves. According to Amy Cuddy's research, changing our body language to include more "power poses" can impact your performance, as well as your success at work, in your relationships, and in all of your endeavors.

Many of the poses involve opening your body and taking up space, making you feel more confident and powerful.

Consider how you feel about yourself when your face is locked in a frown, your arms are crossed defensively, or your body is slumped over. When you smile, stand, or sit up straight, raise your chin, and pull your shoulders back, you feel more positive and self-assured.

Most of us are unconscious of our own body language and the messages we send to others with our facial and physical expressions. But simply by observing other people, you can see how their body language impacts your perceptions of them. The same holds true for you—others do notice, and it makes a difference in how they respond to you.

When you are mindful of your own non-verbal cues, you can change the way others see you and the way you feel about yourself. Amy

Cuddy reminds readers, "Our bodies change our minds, and our minds can change our behavior, and our behavior can change our outcomes."

It only makes sense to focus attention on how you present body language to the world, what you communicate with it, and how your movements and expressions make you feel about yourself.

Action Plan: Find a quiet space where you won't be interrupted. Take a few deep, cleansing breaths, and become aware of your body. Notice how you feel sitting in your chair. Notice any physical sensations, pain, or discomfort.

Perform a quick body scan from head to toe, focusing for a moment on each part of your body so you feel fully grounded in your body.

Notice how you feel emotionally. Are you calm, anxious, stressed, agitated, insecure, bored, ambivalent? Identify your general state of mind as you work through this exercise and begin to change your body position.

Next, notice how you are sitting right now. How is your body positioned? Are you "folded in" and self-protective or open and receptive?

Take a moment to sit up straighter, hold up your chin, push back your shoulders, uncross your arms and legs so your body is in a more powerful, open, and receptive position. Place your hands behind your head, supporting it with your elbows pointing out, and lean back in your chair like a comfortable CEO.

Allow a broad smile to come across your face, as though you are smiling at the warm glow of complete self-assurance and happiness.

Sit in this position for a few minutes and feel yourself opening up to your inner strength, confidence, and joy. Pay attention to how your feelings about yourself might shift as you are physically more open and take up more space. Notice how smiling to yourself changes your state of mind.

After sitting in this position for a few minutes, stand up with your feet shoulder width apart. Maintain the same strong posture with your shoulders back and your chin up. Put your hands on your hips in the "Superman" pose, and smile to yourself again. Then move your arms in a V pose above your head, as though you've just won a big race.

Aside from a little silly, how does this pose make you feel? Envision yourself exuding confidence and magnetism coming out from your chest like a beam of light.

Sit back down and reassess your emotions. How are you feeling right now? Did practicing these poses give you a surge of good feeling? Do you feel more aware of how your body language impacts yourself and others around you?

Before an event or engagement with others in which you want to feel and appear self-assured, go through this exercise again to "prime the pump" for confidence and power.

By practicing power poses daily, you will continue to build your self-confidence and become increasingly mindful of how you present yourself to others.

Learn More: Watch Amy Cuddy's TED Talk on how your body language shapes who you are. Also, check out her book *Presence:*

Bringing Your Boldest Self to Your Biggest Challenges.

If you are interested in learning more about what specific body gestures and positions mean and how they are interpreted by others, read *The Definitive Book of Body Language: The Hidden Meaning Behind People's Gestures and Expressions* by Barbara and Allan Pease.

#51. Take a Laughter Recess

We've all experienced the positive effects of laughter. As the Old Testament reminds, "A merry heart doeth good like a medicine."

Humor allows you to view difficult situations in a more realistic, less daunting light, giving you a psychological distance that helps you cope more effectively.

It also helps you let go of resentments, judgments, criticisms, and doubts. Sharing laughter with others can strengthen your relationships, promote bonding, and diffuse conflict.

It's a universal language recognized by everyone. Whenever Barrie needs a mood boost, she calls her best friend, who knows just what to say to crack her up—and cheer her up at the same time.

Studies show that laughter has some profound physical benefits. It can reduce pain by releasing pain-killing hormones known as endorphins. It also strengthens the immune system with the production of T-cells, interferon, and immune proteins. And it reduces stress by significantly lowering cortisol levels.

Laughter is generally an involuntary response—not something you naturally force yourself to do. It's triggered by mechanisms in your brain and impacts your breathing patterns, facial expressions, and even the muscles in your arms and legs.

As much fun as laughter is, most of our time is spent in more serious or neutral matters, especially during the workday, where maintaining a professional demeanor is required. Life in general often feels very serious. Between the negative news, any personal or professional challenges you might face, and your daily responsibilities, laughter sometimes feels like an indulgence you can't afford.

But taking time in your day for a dose of laughter is a mindfulness habit that is well worth your effort. Says writer, speaker, and cancer survivor Debbie Woodbury in an article for the *Huffington Post*,

> If mindfulness is a state of active, open attention to the present, what is more mindful than laughter? Something strikes you as funny and you laugh. If you analyze it, it's just not funny anymore. For that moment, the laughter and the joy of being in the moment are all you are about. You're like a child again, able to enjoy the moment without quantifying or analyzing your reaction.

Mindfulness doesn't always require focused attention and a disciplined mind. The best kind of present moment awareness is the kind that occurs spontaneously—with a belly laugh attached.

By taking a laughter recess during your day, you give yourself a mental escape that transports you to a higher place where you can enjoy your day from a more relaxed, positive, and joyful perspective.

Action Plan: Laughter is best enjoyed in the company of others, but you can seek out humor on your own to enjoy a few minutes of mindful laughter even when others aren't around.

When you take your laughter break, put away your work, step away from any tasks or projects, turn off your phone (unless you are using it for laughter), and give yourself permission to have fun and enjoy humor.

Here are 11 laughter ideas that you can pursue on your own as a mindfulness habit:

1. Think about a funny event or situation from your life. Close your eyes and relive the moment, allowing yourself to laugh out loud. For example, Barrie's fiancée, Ron, recently dressed up their dog (a Collie) in a down vest. The memory of seeing the dog running around the house in the vest still makes her laugh.

2. Grab a mirror and make silly faces at yourself.

3. Force yourself to laugh in weird ways, and you'll start laughing at yourself for real.

4. Go on YouTube or Facebook to find funny videos and indulge in watching a few that make you laugh out loud. Check out these videos on America's Funniest Home Videos.

5. Check out some humor blogs like Funny or Die and Cracked.

6. Watch a video of someone else laughing, and see how contagious laughter really is.

7. Go to Pandora or iTunes on your computer or phone and type in "comedy" to listen to a few comedians doing sketches.

8. Keep a book of humorous stories or cartoons handy and look through them. One of Barrie's favorite humor authors is David Sedaris, author of *Me Talk Pretty One Day* and *When You Are*

Engulfed In Flames.

9. If you're near a television, turn on a scene from one of your favorite funny movies, or watch reruns of your favorite comedy show that you haven't seen in a while.

10. Create a humorous Pinterest board with some of your favorite cartoons and videos.

11. Put on some fun music and sing and dance to it.

After you finish your laughter habit, take a few deep breaths and assess how you are feeling. Has your mood lightened? Do you feel less stressed? Do you have more energy and motivation to go back to your work or daily activities?

If you choose to make laughter a daily mindfulness habit, pay attention to how it is changing you physically and emotionally. As you see the value in laughter, you'll be inspired to share it with others, which further enhances its positive impact on you.

Learn More: Check out this article on the health benefits of humor and laughter and this article on twenty-two ways to bring more laughter into your life.

You might also enjoy this TED Talk on why we laugh.

#52. Practice a Loving-Kindness Meditation

Your interactions with other people during your day can be a challenge to living mindfully. People often say and do things that push our most sensitive buttons. They can stir the pot of our own insecurities, whether intentionally or not, making it difficult to be fully present and engaged in life and work.

Those around us who are living unconsciously can infect us with their anger, negativity, and resentments. They make it hard for us to respond calmly and thoughtfully. A difficult boss, a jealous coworker, or a passive-aggressive friend can undermine an otherwise calm and happy day.

One of the best ways to protect yourself from the pain of difficult interactions with others is through the practice of a loving-kindness meditation.

Loving-kindness can be defined as non-judgmental, compassion-ate acceptance and awareness of ourselves and others. As Steve and Barrie mention in their book *Declutter Your Mind*, "This kind of meditation cultivates our awareness of others as human beings deserving of compassion and love—even when they are being difficult—which can decrease relationship conflicts and improve your own well-being."

The beauty of a loving-kindness meditation is that it has no conditions. It doesn't matter whether someone "deserves" it or not. Nor is it restricted to your friends and family. Rather, your loving-kindness meditation can extend from people you know to include all sentient beings.

When you practice a loving-kindness meditation, you should have no expectations of anything in return. This meditation is an exercise in unconditional love, something you develop through the daily meditative practice.

Says Steven Smith, a guiding teacher of the Insight Meditation Society, the Kyaswa Retreat Center in Hawaii, "The practice is the softening of the mind and heart, an opening to deeper and deeper levels of the feeling of kindness, of pure love."

Loving-kindness meditation is not simply an exercise in goodwill. It has a profound impact on your relationships and your own outlook. Studies have shown it increases feelings of connectedness with others, as well as boosting feelings of love, joy, contentment, gratitude, pride, hope, interest, amusement, and awe.

It can help you feel more present with others, develop more empathy, and be less reactive to the negative moods of those around you.

Action Plan: Find a quiet place without the possibility of interruption or distraction. Sit in a chair or on the floor in a comfortable posture. Begin with breathing for a few minutes as you would with any meditation.

Pay attention to any areas of mental or emotional distress, self-judgment, or self-hatred. You will begin the loving-kindness meditation by first showing compassion and love to yourself.

As you continue to breathe, speak out loud or to yourself the following phrases:

> » *"May I be free from inner and outer harm and danger."*
> » *"May I be safe and protected."*
> » *"May I be free of mental suffering or distress."*
> » *"May I be happy."*
> » *"May I be free of physical pain and suffering."*
> » *"May I be healthy and strong."*
> » *"May I be able to live in this world happily, peacefully, joyfully, with ease."*

After you speak these phrases for yourself, focus on the person in your life who most invites feelings of pure love—a spouse, parent, or child.

Repeat the same phrase for this person, saying, "May he (or she) be free from inner and outer harm and danger," continuing through each of the statements.

Follow the same exercise for a close friend, then a neutral person (whom you neither like nor dislike), and then for someone who is difficult or causes you resentment or pain. Then end by saying all of the phrases to all beings—"May all beings be happy; may all beings be healthy and strong."

As you repeat the phrase for each person (including yourself), allow the meaning of the phrase to spread through your body like a warm glow. Allow feelings of love, tenderness, and compassion to fill your heart and mind. Try to visualize "loving-kindness" as an invisible force that is activated within you as you practice this meditation.

End the meditation by visualizing all beings on the planet surrounded by a glowing light of love and peace. Take a few deep and cleansing breaths to end the meditation before you return to your day.

Learn More: If you'd like to discover more about the life-changing benefits of practicing loving-kindness, please read *Lovingkindness: The Revolutionary Art of Happiness* by Sharon Salzberg.

You may also enjoy this guided loving-kindness meditation with Tara Branch, founder of the Insight Meditation Community of Washington, DC.

#53. Use ABC Method with Distractions and Interruptions

Distractions are an inevitable part of your day, whether you are trying to focus on a task at work or get something done at home—from paying the bills, to following a recipe, to learning a new skill.

Even if you attempt to reduce potential distractions, your thoughts, emotions, and unexpected interruptions can pull you away from what you are doing and disrupt your flow.

However, you can teach your brain to automatically stop distractions from throwing you off track and hijacking your focus using a simple mindfulness technique call the ABC method.

Action Plan: When you notice a distraction, begin with the "A" of the ABC Method. "A" represents awareness. This allows you to pause whatever you're doing at the moment and recognize the distraction. You might say to yourself, "Here is a distraction, and I have a choice to make."

Next, you implement the "B" of the method, which stands for breathing deeply and reflecting on your options. Do you want to deal with the distraction or interruption right now or dismiss it?

Finally, "C" stands for choosing mindfully how you want to handle the distraction. If you choose to dismiss it, you simply refocus your attention on the task at hand. If you decide to address the distraction or interruption, you are doing so consciously, rather than automatically allowing it to derail you.

Learn More: If you want to strengthen your ability to focus even in the face of distractions, read *The Practicing Mind: Developing Focus and Discipline in Your Life* by Thomas M. Sterner or *Focus: The Hidden Driver of Excellence* by Daniel Goleman.

You might also enjoy this TED Talk on developing focus.

PART VI

EVENING MINDFULNESS HABITS

#54. Mindfully End Your Workday

We have talked a lot about how to be mindful during your day and be more productive and engaged in your work-related tasks. But by the end of the day, you might feel like you need to peel yourself off the floor, drag yourself to the car, and mindlessly make your way home before one more email hits your inbox or one more person asks you to do something.

As the clock gets closer to 5:00 or 6:00, you feel less and less productive, as your mind is taxed from the demands and activities you've been handling for the last seven hours.

However, if you can mindfully bring your workday to completion, you free your mind to transition more easily to your evening routine, and you set yourself up for a more productive and peaceful start to the next day.

Concluding your day in a mindful manner is a vast improvement over what most people do. Even though you may be chomping at the bit to just grab your things and go, taking just ten minutes to close up shop and prepare for tomorrow will give you a sense of renewal that you can carry with you out the door.

Action Plan: Close your eyes, take a few deep breaths, and think about all you have accomplished during the day. Acknowledge to yourself all that you've done today and feel grateful for your productivity.

Make a note about any tasks or projects that you left uncompleted that you need to work on tomorrow. Plan the next day by outlining your calls, activities, and schedule for the day. Be sure to leave room for one or two mindfulness habits during your day. When you plan your day the day before, you're already ahead of the game for when you start work in the morning.

Check your email one last time to see if there's anything you can delete or respond to in five minutes. This helps you reduce your workload in the morning.

Go through the browsers you have open on your computer, and begin to shut things down. Close any files and clean up any items from your computer desktop that need attention. Leave your computer in a way that provides a fresh start in the morning.

Clear off your desk and remove any clutter so you walk in tomorrow morning to a tidy environment.

Before you walk out the door, ask yourself, "Is there anything else I need to do right now? Is there anything I've forgotten?" Sit for a moment to see if any thoughts arise and if there's anything else left to attend to before you leave.

Learn More: Check out this article called "16 Things You Should Do At The End Of Every Work Day," and this one on "How Exceptionally Productive People End The Workday."

#55. Take a Mental Mini-Vacation

As your workday (or your day as a student, parent, or homemaker) comes to a close, your body and mind have accumulated a lot of stress. You may feel exhausted and mentally drained. Even on the best days, you are faced with small challenges, decisions, and aggravations that deplete you.

It's not uncommon to carry that agitation home with you if you don't create a peaceful transition from the demands of your day to the start of your evening. You walk in the door of what should be your sanctuary only to infect your personal environment with the leftover dregs of your daily stress and frustrations.

When Barrie's children were small, she discovered the hard way how they needed a transition from their school day to their after-school activities. They needed an outlet or distraction to allow them to decompress after being mentally "on" all day at school.

As adults, we don't often have the luxury of stopping by the playground on the way home or running around outside with friends. We often move from one set of responsibilities at work to another set at home—taking care of children, preparing meals, and handling chores.

However, you can create a mindful transition from your workday to your home life using a simple visualization practice—a mental vacation. By visualizing your perfect relaxation spot, you can put yourself in a calm, restful, and happy state of mind that allows you to move on peacefully to your next responsibilities.

Action Plan: A great place to conduct your mini-vacation visualization is in your car, just as you are leaving work or at some point before you arrive home. You might pull off in a park or other peaceful setting where you won't be interrupted.

You can also practice this visualization in any space where you have a few minutes of quiet and privacy before you go home from work, or before you transition from your daytime to your evening obligations while already at home.

Close your eyes and practice some calming breaths to get into a more relaxed frame of mind. You might breathe for several counts of ten until you feel your body unwinding and your mind releasing the day's demands and stresses. Allow your body to sink further and further into deep relaxation.

Next, think about a place where you feel completely happy, calm, and relaxed. This could be a place where you have vacationed in the past or a place you simply imagine.

You might think about sitting on a beautiful beach at sunset, watching the waves. Or you could image sitting in a lush, quiet forest by a soothing stream as water burbles over rocks.

Whatever your peaceful place happens to be, you want to mentally immerse yourself in it using all your senses. If you are at the beach, for example, notice the way the sun glints on the water and how blue the sky and ocean are.

Feel the waves washing over your feet and the warm sand underneath you. Listen to the sounds of the waves crashing on the shore, the seagulls calling, and the children playing farther down the beach. Smell the salt air and the suntan lotion you put on your body earlier.

Visualize the setting in minute detail, paying attention to the positive feelings the setting evokes for you. Mentally step outside of yourself for a moment, and view yourself in this vacation setting. What are you doing? Notice how calm and relaxed you look and how happy you appear. Let a smile spread on your face as you look at yourself feeling so great.

Visualize the calming energy of this beautiful spot as a white light that surrounds your body and slowly seeps inside of you. Now you can carry the peace and joy of this mini-vacation spot with you as you return to the next part of your day.

Look around you one more time, knowing that you can come back to this spot any time you wish. Take a few more deep breaths, and open your eyes.

Learn More: Enjoy this guided visualization that takes you on a walk along the beach, and this one that takes you on a walk in the forest.

You might also enjoy this twenty-minute Secret Garden guided meditation.

#56. Give Yourself a Mindfulness Massage

Your body is intricately connected to your mental and emotional state. If your day has been demanding and stressful, or if you've been dealing with long-term stress related to a life challenge, you are bound to notice some unpleasant physical reactions.

Says author and physician Bernie Siegal, MD, "The mind and body are not separate units, but one integrated system. How we act and what we think, eat, and feel are all related to our health."

By paying attention to your body and noticing where you feel discomfort, you can address both the pain, as well as the source of the stress that caused it.

One place stress appears in your body is in your muscles. You may notice your muscles feel tight, spasm, ache, or have persistent pain.

Muscle pain can be exacerbated if you lean over a computer all day or do physical work where you overuse a muscle group.

Barrie carries stress and muscle pain in her neck and shoulders, as she spends many hours a day working at her computer. But muscle pain from stress can affect any muscle group and even migrate from one area to another. You might feel it in your jaw, face, back of your head, chest, arms, legs, and feet, in addition to your shoulders and neck.

When you're stressed or anxious, your body secretes stress hormones into your bloodstream, which travel to different parts of your body. They are released to prepare your body for the fight-or-flight response to a perceived threat.

One of the responses these hormones stimulate is the contraction of muscles. Muscles contract to make the body more resilient to a potential attack. However, most of our stressors aren't physical threats—they are thoughts and feelings. But, nonetheless, the muscles remain in a state of emergency readiness, contracted and tight.

As a result, you might experience headaches, muscle stiffness, pain, and tension, which are common symptoms of stress-response hyper-stimulation in your muscles. In addition, stress and anxiety can also impact the body's ability to regulate pain, making muscle pain even more pronounced.

Massage therapy is one of the best-known treatments for muscle tension. It gets directly to the muscle tissue, allowing the muscle to release its contraction and ease the pain. It also induces the "relaxation response" in which your heart rate slows, your blood pressure decreases, and you produce less of the stress hormones. Finally, massage can improve blood circulation and reduce nerve compression.

You may not have the time or money to go to a massage therapist every day, but you can give yourself a daily massage and enjoy many of the same benefits. In fact, through self-massage, you will get to know your own muscle "trigger" points where tension and stress are stored and learn how to ease the muscle contraction while being mindful of the sources of your stress.

Action Plan: Sit in a chair or on the floor in a comfortable position. Begin with a few minutes of mindful breathing to get into a more relaxed frame of mind.

Starting at the top of your head, mentally scan down the length of your body, noticing any areas of pain, muscle tension, or discomfort. When you encounter an area of pain, ask yourself, "What is the source of this discomfort?" Wait a few seconds to see if an answer arises.

The answer may be as innocuous as pain from bending over your computer. Or it could be stored tension from an argument with someone or an emotional issue you haven't resolved. You may not get any answer, but sit with it to see if you can uncover the cause. If you do, make a mental note of it.

After you perform the body scan, you can begin your self-massage. When you reach any of the pain points on your body, pay close attention to these areas during your massage. Be sure to breathe into any discomfort as your perform the massage.

Here are the five areas where you can focus your efforts:

1. Head and Face

Begin at the crown of your head by placing your hands on either side and massaging your scalp. Continue to move your hands down the back and sides of your head, using your thumbs to massage the base of your head at the top of your spine. Then move your thumbs to your temples and gently massage all around them.

Use your fingers to massage your forehead, eyebrows, and the space between your eyebrows that gets furrowed and tight when you feel worried. Raise your eyebrows up and down several times.

Use your fingers to gently massage all around your eyes, your nose, and your cheeks. Then use your index and middle fingers to massage your jaw area. Open your mouth and jaw as wide as possible several times to stretch your jaw, which is another area that tends to hold tension.

Grab an ear in each hand and gently massage your ears and the area around your ears.

2. Neck and Shoulders

Reach around to the back of your neck, and place your fingers on either side. With light pressure, walk your fingers up and down your neck. Gently bend your head from side to side, as though you are trying to touch your ear to your shoulder.

Move your hands to your shoulders and your trapezius muscles and use your fingers to apply gentle pressure and massage. Reach as far down your back as you can and continue massaging, using as much pressure as feels comfortable to you.

3. Arms and Hands

Using your opposite hand, reach over to your other arm and begin massaging your upper arm, starting at your shoulder and working your way down to your hand. Then massage the palm of your hand using your thumb. Massage each individual finger, pulling on them slightly as you rub away from your hand.

Switch to the other arm and follow the same instructions.

4. Torso

Next, focus on the muscles in your chest, massaging in small concentric circles from your armpit area to the center of your chest. Reach your arms behind you as if you're trying to clasp your hands to stretch the muscles in your chest area.

Bend at the waist to the left and right, stretching your rib muscles. Then gently massage your abdominal muscles.

Reach behind you to your lower back, and use your fingers and the heel of your hand to massage the muscles around your lower spine and hips. Move to your buttocks and massage your gluteal muscles.

5. Legs and Feet

Loosen up tight quads by massaging your thighs with the heel of your hand (or use a tennis ball or foam roller), working your way down your thighs in small circles. Then use your hands and thumbs to knead your calf muscles, working down to your ankles. Massage the muscles around your Achilles tendon and heel, moving to the sole of your feet. Use your thumb, the heel of your hand, or a tennis ball to massage the entire surface of your foot.

Grab each of your toes and flex them back while applying a gentle stretch with your hands. Then gently rub each of your toes.

Completing the Mindful Massage

Once you finish your mini-massage, close your eyes, take a few deep breaths, and pay attention to how you feel. Are you more relaxed and calm? Do your muscles feel less tense and contracted? Do you feel less stressed in general?

Perform a body scan one more time to see if there are areas where you still feel discomfort. You might want to massage those spots more, or consider getting a professional massage to release the tension in the muscles.

To end the session, mentally review the sources of your tension and stress. Think about any changes in your behavior, reactions, mind-set, or lifestyle that might help reduce your stress so that you carry less of it in your body.

#57. Reconnect with Your Relationships

The people we care about—our spouse, children, family members, and friends—often give us a sense of purpose and connection. They provide the love, support, and affection that we all crave to live happily. Without these important people, we would feel a vacuum, no matter how successful or productive we may be otherwise.

Close relationships have the added benefit of improving our physical health and well-being. Studies confirm that having relationships can make you live longer, reduce feelings of stress, and improve your overall happiness.

Says Marcel Proust, "Let us be grateful to people who make us happy, they are the charming gardeners who make our souls blossom." But you may have discovered how easy it is to take these charming gardeners for granted—to put them behind your work, your obligations, and even your distractions.

At the end of a stressful day, you may be diverted from your family by the lure of your smartphone or computer. You may be in such a hurry to get dinner on the table that you ignore your child's longing for a few minutes of your time. You may feel so exhausted that you neglect to return your mom's call or acknowledge your friend's attempts to connect with you.

It is ironic that we place such high value on relationships, but we have trouble prioritizing them in our lives. In her book *The Top Five Regrets of the Dying: A Life Transformed by the Dearly Departing*, author and palliative care nurse Bronnie Ware shares the most common deathbed regrets. Two of the five regrets related to missing out on time with family and friends due to the distractions of work and life.

When all else falls away, our relationships are one of the few things that really matter. Nurturing these important relationships requires your mindful daily attention. Your spouse (or partner), children, family, and friends need your time and presence, and you need theirs to truly feel fulfilled in life.

One of the obvious times to reconnect with your loved ones is at the end of the day when your family is in the home together again.

By carving out "reconnection time" with your family members, you take charge of your happiness and emotional well-being. You are strengthening bonds that will allow you to look back on your life with gratitude rather than regret.

Action Plan: There are four ways to mindfully reconnect with your relationships:

1. Recommit to the value of your relationships.

Before you walk in the door, think about your values and life priorities. Your family (and friends) should be at the top of the list, and you may need a moment to remind yourself of this. Commit to making time to reconnect with them at the end of the day.

2. Set aside time with your spouse or partner first.

Your marriage or love relationship must be the centerpiece of your family. When this relationship is strong, it makes your children feel secure and loved. Before you get involved with chores or pulled away by children, reconnect with your partner first—as soon as possible after you are both home in the early evening.

Take a few minutes to sit down or take a short walk to discuss the events of the day, to hug and cuddle, and to enjoy some quiet reconnection time by yourselves. Leave your phone and computer behind so you aren't tempted to take a peek.

Practice active listening, being fully present with your spouse without distraction. Look into your partner's eyes, feeling your love for him or her deeply. Ask questions or reflect back what your partner has said to show your engagement in the conversation.

Just ten minutes of time together will give you both a sense of calm and connection that can help you let go of stress and have more energy to tackle evening responsibilities.

3. Reconnect with your children.

Being present with your children doesn't have to be complicated or overscheduled. It simply requires you to be fully engaged with them in whatever they are doing, even if it's for just a few minutes.

Take ten minutes to sit down with your child at the end of the day, without your phones or other electronics. Inquire about your child's day, how they are feeling, and what they have going on in their world. Listen attentively and respond thoughtfully to your child. If they are small enough, pull them onto your lap while you talk and offer physical affection.

If your child doesn't feel like talking, play a game or read a book together. Or go outside and throw a ball, push them on a swing, or just take a short walk. If your child is already engaged in an activity, join in and participate with enthusiasm.

Give your child your full attention so he or she knows you are in the here and now with them—not distracted by work, chores, or other life demands. Look them in the eyes and give them a warm smile. Your loving presence gives your child the security and comfort to come to you in the future, during good times and bad, knowing you are available for them.

4. Reconnect with other family members or friends.

If you live alone, it is still valuable to reconnect with the important people in your life at the end of the day. By mindfully nurturing your relationships, you are taking action to improve your life satisfaction and well-being.

Take ten minutes to call your parents, a sibling, a relative, or a close friend. Inquire about how they are doing. Let them know how much you care about them. Make an arrangement to spend time together.

Remind yourself how important these relationships are in your life and how you don't want them to slip away. Even if you aren't able to talk to your friends or family, maintaining a feeling of gratitude for their presence in your life will help you relieve stress and feel positive about your quality of life.

Learn More: While the book *Anxious in Love* specializes in helping readers reconnect with their partner, there are many good ideas that you can use to reestablish the other relationships in your life.

#58. Practice Walking Meditation

A walking meditation is an active mindfulness habit where you are moving in the environment. Rather than sitting in a chair or on a cushion on the floor, you are outside, getting movement with your eyes and senses open.

Unlike seated meditation in which you are withdrawn into yourself and your breathing, a walking meditation requires engaging all your senses. You are intentionally aware of your feet hitting the ground, your eyes taking in the sights around you, your lungs breathing the air in and out, and your ears hearing every sound.

It's a practice that allows you to be more connected with the environment, which is an essential part of who we are. Being in nature releases you from the ongoing internal dialogue of your mind and makes you more aware of the beauty of the outdoors.

By combining walking with mindfulness, you are practicing an excellent habit for releasing the stress of the day so you can transition to your evening activities in a more harmonious frame of mind.

Action Plan: Find a place outside where you can practice your walking meditation without being interrupted by other people. It might be a quiet park or a path near your home.

Before starting, spend a minute or two breathing deeply and anchoring your attention in your body. Stand up straight, and keep your gaze somewhat down to help with concentration. Place your feet hip-width apart so your weight is balanced evenly on both feet. Consciously feel the stability of the ground beneath your feet.

As author and Buddhist teacher Jack Kornfield says, "Let yourself walk with a sense of ease and dignity. Relax and let your walking be easy and natural, as if you were a king or queen out for a royal stroll."

Next, close your eyes and take a few deep breaths. Scan your entire body from feet to head, making note of any discomfort, sensations, thoughts, or feelings. Bring your awareness fully to your body and your physical presence in the environment.

Begin walking forward slowly, one foot in front of the other. Pay attention to lifting each foot and placing it on the ground. Notice how your heel hits the ground before your toes. Notice how the ground feels beneath your foot.

Take several steps this way, paying mindful attention to each step. If your mind wanders, just bring it back to your steps. You might want to count each step to keep your mind focused as you walk, or you could use a short verse that you repeat, like "I am here," or "I am walking." Keep your breathing slow and relaxed.

After a few steps, stop for a moment and notice your environment. Look at the trees, the grass, and the sky. Feel the warm or cool air on your face and skin. Listen intently to the sounds of nature, and pay attention to any smells or scents you notice. Notice your body again and any sensations you are experiencing. Pay attention to your thoughts for a moment and watch them float past without attachment or judgment.

If you want to keep your walk to ten minutes, you may need to turn around and begin walking back. Return to your meditative walking, noticing each step with engaged attention.

When your walking meditation comes to a close, gently stop walking and notice your surroundings again, using all of your senses. Take a few deep breaths and return to your regular activities.

Learn More: If you'd like to learn more about different types of walking meditation, please read this article called "The Ultimate Guide to Walking Meditation."

#59. Create a Dinner Ritual

Rituals are actions we imbue with meaning and significance that enhance our lives in some way. They are performed in a prescribed way that lends an element of sacredness to the occasion. You likely experience many rituals related to religious holidays, family gatherings, or birthday celebrations.

When Barrie's children were young, she and her husband created Christmas morning rituals that required the kids to wait in anxious anticipation while the Christmas tree was lit, the music was turned on, breakfast was put in the oven, and the video recorder was prepared for filming. These actions were followed by the kids racing downstairs to first see their "Santa" gifts, then look in their stockings, and finally open the gifts under the tree. The routine never changed.

Rituals have played a role in human social existence from the time of the earliest primitive societies to our modern rituals around sports, celebrating the New Year, or carving the Thanksgiving turkey.

Says Kevin Carrico in an article in *Cultural Anthropology*, "Ritual is in fact an inevitable component of culture, extending from the largest-scale social and political processes to the most intimate aspects of our self-experience."

Rituals provide structure and stability in our otherwise random lives, and they foster deeper connections with the people we love. They help us celebrate our values in a meaningful way. They solidify commitments and reinforce beliefs. And they inspire us to feel gratitude for the occasion they are built around.

A recent study has shown that rituals around food even make it taste more flavorful and worthy of savoring. In fact, the delay between the ritual and the consumption heightened the enjoyment of the food.

Creating a ritual around the evening meal is an ideal mindfulness habit to establish with your family. It blends all of these benefits into an occasion that is celebrated nightly but can yield a lifetime of memories and closeness for you and your children.

It's so easy to allow the family dinner to fall by the wayside. Between busy schedules, extracurricular activities, and the convenience of fast food and microwavable meals, the sit-down family dinner has become more the exception than the norm. But it's a tradition well worth resurrecting.

According to a recent article in the *New York Times*,

> A 2004 study of 4,746 children 11 to 18 years old, published in *The Archives of Pediatrics and Adolescent Medicine*, found that frequent family meals were associated with a lower risk of smoking, drinking and using marijuana; with a lower incidence of depressive symptoms and suicidal thoughts; and with better grades.

A dinner ritual reconnects your family each evening in a powerful way, helping each member focus on celebrating your familial love. It offers a sacred respite from the pressures of work, school, and life in general, especially if you reinforce that the dinner table is an inviolable space where negativity and distractions are not allowed.

Action Plan: There are so many ways to create a mindful dinner ritual with your family, and none of them need to be costly, elaborate, or time-consuming. The important part of this ritual is bringing your family together in a way that makes the meal feel meaningful.

Although preparing a meal and sitting down with your family to eat it is a practice that will take more than ten minutes, it shouldn't take much more than that. Determine what your dinnertime rituals will be and communicate them to your family.

Here are six ideas that both Steve and Barrie have used to create a quality evening tradition.

1. Communicate your intentions.

Let your spouse and children know that you want to create a mindfulness habit around your evening meal. Talk with them about the benefits of sitting down together as a family, even if it's just for a few nights a week. Ask them for ideas and input on what would make the mealtime special. Make sure everyone understands and agrees to the rules of the evening ritual.

2. Get the entire family involved.

Rather than it falling just on mom or dad to prepare the evening meal, make it a family event. Young children can help with easy food prep and setting the table. Older kids can make a salad, cook pasta, or help with chopping. The meal doesn't need to be complicated or fancy. You can establish a lovely dinner ritual around the simplest meals.

3. Create a special environment.

Light candles at the dinner table. Put on relaxing music. Dim the lights to create a calm mood. Turn off the television and ban smartphones from the table. Make sure everyone is seated before beginning the meal, and make sure no one leaves the table without asking to be excused. Set the stage for a calm and positive connection when everyone sits down to eat.

4. Establish a ritual before eating.

Whether it's saying a family prayer before eating or just taking a moment to express gratitude, a mindful acknowledgement of the blessings of the food before you and what was involved in its preparation is a lovely ritual to establish. This allows your family to appreciate how bountiful healthy food is in your home, and the effort involved in growing and preparing the food.

5. Create a positive and light atmosphere.

It may be tempting to use the dinner hour as a time to lecture kids on good manners, discuss the latest political issues, or share your frustrations about your difficult boss. But, instead, keep this special time sacred by making it upbeat and light.

Tell funny stories or share good memories. Talk to your children about what you love and appreciate about them. Ask questions that invite conversation. Try not to let one or two family members dominate the conversation by making sure everyone has a chance to talk. You might go around the table, allowing each person to share one thing they are grateful for or one fun thing they experienced during the day.

6. Be creative and open.

Your dinnertime traditions and rituals can shift and change. Maybe you want to include grandparents on Sunday nights. As your kids get older, you may need to change the dinner hour to accommodate busy schedules. You may want to establish one night as "pizza night" where you order in—but still sit down together as a family. The most important part of this mindfulness practice is togetherness and gratitude.

Learn More: If you'd like to create more family rituals, check out the book, *How to Celebrate Everything: Recipes and Rituals for Birthdays, Holidays, Family Dinners, and Every Day In Between* by Jenny Rosenstrach.

Also read this article with over sixty ideas for creating family traditions from the blog *The Art of Manliness*.

#60. Wash Dishes Mindfully

After a mindful dinner with your family, the reality of your nightly responsibilities sets in. The table is cluttered with dirty dishes, and the sink is filled with messy pots and pans. Getting your family to chip in and help clean up after dinner is ideal, but sometimes you are left to handle the mess yourself.

Not many people savor the effort of washing dishes, especially doing them by hand without a dishwasher. Next to cleaning the bathroom, washing dishes is one of the most despised chores. However, dishwashing is a mindfulness habit that is far underrated. In fact, a recent study showed that washing dishes can significantly lower stress levels if the effort is done mindfully.

In the study, participants were asked to read the following passage before they began washing the dishes:

> While washing the dishes one should only be washing the dishes. This means that while washing the dishes one should be completely aware of the fact that one is washing the dishes. At first glance, that might seem a little silly. Why put so much

stress on a simple thing? But that's precisely the point. The fact that I am standing there and washing is a wondrous reality. I'm being completely myself, following my breath, conscious of my presence, and conscious of my thoughts and actions. There's no way I can be tossed around mindlessly like a bottle slapped here and there on the waves.

The participants who followed the mindfulness guidelines in washing dishes showed a marked increase in their feelings of inspiration and a decrease in stress compared with the participants who washed dishes without using mindfulness.

Mundane chores that require little concentration can be used as a time of respite from your looping and stress-filled thoughts—if the chore is done mindfully. Doing this task slowly and mindfully allows you to appreciate simple pleasures and see the beauty in everyday efforts that are a necessary part of life.

Says Buddhist monk Thích Nhất Hạnh, "If while washing dishes, we think only of the cup of tea that awaits us, thus hurrying to get the dishes out of the way as if they were a nuisance, then we are not 'washing the dishes to wash the dishes.' What's more, we are not alive during the time we are washing the dishes."

You may not want to hand wash dishes every night, but creating a mindfulness habit around this task (with or without a dishwasher) will not only enhance the experience, but it will also inspire you to continue in a state of mindfulness for the rest of your evening.

Action Plan: Stand at your sink, close your eyes, and take a deep breath to help you get into a more mindful and relaxed state of mind.

Clean out your sink, and place all the dishes, utensils, pots, and pans beside the sink. Begin scraping all of the solid bits of uneaten food into the trash or disposal, or if you have a pet or a compost pile, save the appropriate scraps. As you scrape the dishes, focus on your gratitude for the meal you just consumed.

Once the dishes are scraped, fill your sink with hot soapy water. Feel gratitude for the immediate availability of clean water. Notice the feel of the water and the bubbles arising from the dish soap. Set out a dish rack or towel to place the clean dishes on. Or you may want to place them in the dishwasher.

Begin washing the dishes one at a time, starting with the less oily or messy dishes to keep the water cleaner for longer. Immerse the dish in the soapy water, and notice how the warm water feels on your hands. Use a sponge or towel to clean the dish thoroughly, taking your time to ensure you remove all remnants of food and oil.

Turn on the warm water and rinse each dish, paying attention to the feeling of the water and the way the soapy water runs off it. Notice how the soap smells and how the clean plate shines in the light. Gently place it on the rack, towel, or in the dishwasher.

Continue washing each dish and utensil this way, noticing every action and sensation along the way. Be fully present and aware of washing the dishes. If your mind wanders, gently bring it back to the task at hand.

If you have a lot of dishes and pans, and the water is getting murky, you may need to drain the water and begin again with clean water and soap.

Continue to clean all your dishes mindfully, and then watch as the water slowly drains from the sink after you are finished. You may want to let the dishes dry on the rack or in the dishwasher. Or you may want to continue this mindfulness task and dry them by hand, paying full attention to the drying cloth, the dish, and the effort to put the dish away.

Once you are completely done, take a deep breath and appreciate your clean dishes, the clean sink, and the clean counter. Congratulate yourself for handling this task with mindfulness.

Learn More: Discover how to bring mindfulness into your ordinary daily life with the book *Bringing Home the Dharma: Awakening Right Where You Are* by Jack Kornfield.

#61. Create a Task Ritual

Washing the dishes at the end of your evening meal is probably not the only task you have on your plate as you wind down for the night. You may need to wash and fold a few loads of laundry, mow the lawn, bathe children, or handle other chores around the house.

After a long day, you might feel resentful about these extra chores and try to rush through them so you can finally relax. But there is a more mindful way to tackle your tasks and maybe even enjoy them.

Consider the Zen proverb: "Before enlightenment, chop wood, carry water. After enlightenment, chop wood, carry water." The idea is that we can find meaning in ordinary tasks because mindfulness transforms your labor from a burden to a time of peace and contentment.

The notion of finding meaning in simple tasks is not just a Buddhist tradition; it's part of many religious traditions. Christians consider cleanliness next to godliness. Benedictines see prayer and work as inseparable. Jews must clean their homes as part of the preparation for the Sabbath.

The simple tasks of running your daily household are the bread of life and even sustenance for the soul. They are essential to you maintaining your lifestyle and should be viewed as a valuable contribution to the happiness and well-being of everyone in your home.

When you perform these tasks with the goal of rushing to get them over with, you're not only creating anxiety and distraction for yourself, but you are also telegraphing your resentment to those you love. When your work is done with resentment, it poisons the fruits of your labor and creates unease for you and those around you.

Instead of just "getting the job done," you can ritualize your tasks, transforming them from menial dreaded chores to sacred moments of love and attention. Says Zen teacher and writer Karen Maezen Miller, "Your own attention is what spiritualizes things. Attention to the meal you cook, the clothes you wash. Attention is love. And that's transformative."

This act of paying attention while completing chores is a way of practicing "zazen" where you lose the conscious mind through repetitive action. The more you practice zazen by focusing on the task at hand, the easier it becomes and the more contentment and peace you will feel. With practice, your chores will take on deeper purpose, and over time you will find even the most menial tasks worthwhile.

Action Plan: Before you begin any task around your house, take a few minutes to think about why you are doing the task, how it connects to your values, and how it makes a positive difference for you and your family. You may want to write down your thoughts so you can refer back to them.

For example, if you are folding laundry, you might write that you are doing this task so you and your family have fresh, clean clothes to wear during the week. You value cleanliness and comfort, and you want your family (and yourself) to enjoy the pleasure of having clean clothes readily available. Having a purpose in mind before you begin a task helps you complete it with more motivation and awareness, rather than simply performing a rote activity.

Whatever the task happens to be, turn it into a ritual by setting the scene in a way that increases your comfort and enjoyment as well as your sense of the sacred in the task. Prepare your supplies. Set up the space where you will work. Adjust the lighting. Turn on some music that is peaceful and calming. Remove distractions like your phone, computer, or television so you can be fully engaged in the experience.

As you begin the task, take a moment to feel gratitude for whatever it is you are working on—the clothes you are folding, the tub you are cleaning that provides a space for bathing, the beautiful grass you have to mow. Remind yourself of the purpose for this task and how the outcome will add to your well-being.

View the task as a form of meditation. Stay with the actions of the task as you would follow your breathing in meditation. Notice the sensations involved in the task and how your body feels performing it. If your mind wanders, gently bring it back to your actions involved in the work you are doing.

Perform the job slowly and carefully, being as thorough as possible. If you are trying to keep the task to ten minutes, consider breaking up larger tasks so you have more than one evening to complete them.

When you complete your work, step back and acknowledge what you have done. Feel proud of your finished product and the effort you expended to make it happen.

Learn More: You might enjoy this article on "What the Buddhists Can Teach Us About Household Chores." Also, here is an excellent article on performing tasks mindfully called "12 Essential Rules to Live More Like a Zen Monk."

#62. Engage in Handwork

Handwork is any kind of work or hobby that involves using your hands and some level of concentration. A few examples of handwork might be knitting, needlework, embroidery, weaving, crochet, beading, origami, mosaic art, wirework, whittling, soap carving, quilting, bookmaking, and calligraphy.

Through the practice of handwork, you develop a connection between the sensorial experience, mental focus, and the act of creation. The focus required isn't so complex that it's overly challenging. On the contrary, these activities can be deeply relaxing and fulfilling.

For instance, Steve's grandfather liked to spend his free time carving wooden duck decoys. It was his way of relaxing and unwinding after a long day of work. One of Steve's earliest childhood memories was sitting on the stairs, watching his grandfather delicately craft each decoy. Now, whenever he sees one of his grandfather's decoys in his office, Steve thinks of his grandfather and his enjoyment of handwork.

Action Plan: Learning handwork is like building any other skill-based habit. You begin by understanding the process, then you commit to working at it daily, and finally, you create small milestones that you use to work toward mastery. Here is a brief overview of how to get started with developing a handwork skill.

First, pick a single skill that you'd like to master. Our suggestion is to identify something you've always wanted to learn and then completely immerse yourself in this area. That's the secret to quickly achieving expert status. If you get stuck, here is an extensive list of different crafts you can learn.

Next, you should do a complete deep-dive on this subject to learn everything you can about this skill.

To get started, I recommend the following six actions to find the best resources for your chosen skill:

1. **Buy or borrow top-rated books.** Start with a Google search to identify the books most recommended by experts in this industry. Then go to Amazon, a local library, or Audible (if you prefer audiobooks) to grab a copy. (I recommend using the interlibrary system because it's convenient *and* free.) If you're not sure where to get started, you can begin with something in the *For Dummies* or *Complete Idiot's Guide To* series.

2. **Listen to multiple podcasts.** Download the Stitcher app, search for niche-specific podcasts, and listen to a few episodes from each one. When you find a few favorites, use Stitcher to

organize them into a playlist that is streamed directly into your queue. Listen to these shows during those pockets of time that would normally be wasted (like driving or running errands).

3. **Watch video tutorials if you need a demonstration for a technical or mechanical skill.** Start with YouTube and look for channels that focus on a single topic. If you need additional instructions, sign up for a course on sites like Lynda, Udemy, CreativeLive, Coursera, edX, or Masterclass. Finally, use TED Talks to expand your thinking on what you're learning.

4. **Learn in a real-world setting.** Attend classes provided by chain stores, community colleges, or your local library. If you want to quickly achieve mastery, hire a private coach who can get you past those initial roadblocks and challenges.

5. **Learn online.** Read niche-related blogs and interact with others through forums and Facebook groups. Plus, consider starting a podcast if you want to connect with top authorities in your area of expertise.

6. **Purchase a how-to course.** If you feel stuck or simply want a shortcut to learn as much as possible in a short amount of time, this type of course will jumpstart you.

Finally, set aside at least ten minutes daily to work on your budding handcraft skills. During this time, we recommend an eight-step process:

1. **Understand the fundamentals.** Identify the critical components, or get a recommendation (from a coach) for specific drills to focus on.

2. **Practice (and master) each microcomponent.** Your goal is to master each aspect of the skill in one to three sessions. If you

can't master it during this time, then look for a way to further drill down the skill into a smaller component.

3. **Get immediate feedback from a skill expert.** If you can hire a coach, then this will be a worthwhile investment. Otherwise, find videos of someone demonstrating this skill and ask a friend to provide a critique based on what you see.

4. **Embrace your mistakes.** Don't be afraid to make a mistake during these sessions. Sure, it might not be fun to make errors, but just remember this is an important part of the learning process.

5. **Slow down your deliberate practice.** You don't need to rush through a skill to master it. In fact, it's better to go as slowly as possible to understand how it works and then increase your speed as you start to achieve mastery.

6. **Complete many repetitions.** Doing the same thing over and over will build the muscle memory that's an important part of turning a skill into an unconscious action. In addition, you should consider increasing the difficulty of these practice sessions, so you perform well no matter what comes up.

7. **Take breaks during your practice session.** You'll find it's easier to retain information and master a skill by breaking down a session into smaller segments with quick breaks. I recommend the Pomodoro Technique, where you work for twenty-five minutes, rest for five, and then work for another twenty-five minutes. Repeat this process as often as you need.

8. **Track your success.** Record your progress in a journal and be honest about any challenges you're experiencing. My suggestion is to use a tool like The Freedom Journal.

You'll discover it's not hard to pick up a handwork skill if you break down the process into small components and then master each one.

Learn More: Steve's book *Novice to Expert* will teach you the process of how to systematically break down a new skill and work at it as a daily habit.

#63. Give Yourself a Break from Television

The television has become a constant companion and source of entertainment in most households. The average adult in the United States watches more than four hours of television a day. That's about a quarter of your waking time each day or about three extra months per year.

Although it might seem like a nightly relaxation ritual, watching television can add to your stress because it pulls you away from other things you could or should be doing—things that are better for your mental and physical health.

Studies show that those who watch television for three hours or more a day have a greater chance of being obese than those who watch less than an hour of daily TV.

Not only are we sedentary while watching television, but we also tend to eat and snack mindlessly. We aren't counting the number of times our hands reach into the bag of chips or how many cookies we've just consumed.

Television is distracting and can be emotionally draining. While you watch TV, your mind is receiving stimuli that you have to process. Much of that stimuli is mind-numbing at best and often quite distressing.

In fact, heavy television users report feeling less happy and more anxious than light users. The heavy users said their mood deteriorated after watching TV compared to how they felt before watching. Professors at the University of Maryland also discovered through a study that unhappy people watch up to 30 percent more television than happy people.

Although many TV programs are educational and positive, excessive watching can have a particularly negative impact on children, affecting their grades, sleep habits, and behavior.

You can certainly enjoy watching television programs as a family, and you may even have a ritual of watching certain programs together. But watching TV together is not the same as being present for one another. It's hard to feel connected when all eyes and ears are glued to a box.

Taking a respite from your television creates so many opportunities for mindfulness—both as a family and as individuals. You'll have more time to connect with your spouse and children. You can reengage in hobbies and interests you might have put on the shelf. You can work on projects, meditate, exercise, or learn a new skill instead of engaging in passive, mind-numbing entertainment.

If television is a big part of your nightly activities, you may need to slowly wean yourself back from it, as it does have an addictive quality. Perhaps you turn it off during dinner, or wait a while before you click the "On" button. Use this time for a mindful activity that can help you unwind and relax.

When you wean back on your television consumption, you are also compelled to be more mindful about what you *do* watch. Some television is engaging and educational, but the average haphazard TV diet contains way too much junk. Rather than just turning on the set and watching whatever happens to be on, you can make thoughtful choices that align with your values.

Stepping away from the TV allows you to be more fully alive. Sitting passively in front of an entertainment box is not really living. Rather than watching others taking action and enjoying life, you and your family can reclaim some of that time to enjoy more of it yourselves.

Action Plan: Start by getting real about how much time you and your family spend in front of the television. Mentally review the last week and the number of hours the TV was turned on. A dose of reality can be a big motivator to cut back and be more mindful about how you spend your time.

Sit down with your spouse and family to talk about your desire to cut back on watching television. Explain to them the negative effects of watching a lot of TV and the benefits of turning it off. Make sure you and your spouse agree about cutting back before you present the idea to your children.

Decide on the amount of television time you want to reduce or the number of shows you can cut out each evening. If you watch a lot of TV, start small so you don't suffer from too much "television withdrawal." You might consider turning it off thirty minutes earlier each night, or maybe you decide to turn it off during meals.

Also make a thoughtful decision about the TV programs you want to watch, rather than indiscriminately watching whatever happens to be on. There are certain types of shows that seem to be more addictive, time-consuming, and negative than others. You might consider dropping reality TV, talking-head news programs, three-hour sports shows, or programs with a lot of violence.

Think about positive ways you can fill the television void during the time you've turned it off. Try not to use that time for chores or anything you (or your kids) resist, as you won't be motivated to keep the TV off. Use the time for a relaxing hobby or to read a book. You might play a game with your family, take an evening walk, or work on a creative project together.

Notice how you feel as you cut back on television watching. You may find you are more agitated or bored without the background noise of the television. You may even crave turning it back on. Notice these feelings, but let them pass without immediately reaching for the remote. Instead, refocus your attention on the present moment and what you are (or could be) doing to replace TV watching.

Pay attention to sensations you often miss when focusing on a television show—the sounds of your house settling, the way the light plays in your home, or the peace of having the family pet nearby.

After a few weeks of cutting back on television, check in again to see how you and your family feel about dedicating time for more mindful activities. Talk about the positive impact of spending more time together and doing things that are more engaging and positive.

If this television respite has been positive for you, consider further reducing the amount of time you watch it. Try to get to the point where watching a TV program is a special event rather than a daily routine.

Learn More: If you'd like more ideas on what you can do instead of watching television, check out this list of 59 ideas.

You might also enjoy this TED Talk on the value of trying something new for thirty days.

#64. Develop a Mindful Parenting Plan

Mindful parenting isn't just a positive catchphrase. Children who experience this form of parent have distinct advantages like avoiding depression, anxiety, acting out, and drug use.

In fact, a University of Vermont study looked at how mindful and positive parenting impacted the well-being of the children involved in the study. They defined mindful parenting as how attentive, non-judging, and non-reacting the parents were in interactions with their children. Positive parenting includes actions like expressing unconditional love and setting limits versus using harsh physical punishments.

The positive and mindful parenting approach was linked with more positive behavior from the children. The kids acted out less and experienced less anxiety and depression.

According to the study, there are three critical factors involved in mindful parenting:

1. Being aware of your own feelings during a conflict with your child.

2. Taking a pause when you are angry before responding to your child.

3. Listening attentively to your child's opinion even when you disagree with it.

Although mindful parenting has a profound impact on children, parents often get tripped up in the heat of the moment. Maintaining your patience when a child acts out can be a real challenge, even when you have the best intentions in mind.

With our busy, hectic lives, it's hard to be calm when things start to get crazy with your kids. The goal of mindful parenting isn't to be a perfect parent who never reacts, but instead to have a goal for being more present and responsive with your children, even though you may fail at times.

Says Jon Kabat-Zinn in an interview for Gaiam:

> Mindful parenting is a lifelong practice. It means you become less attached to outcomes and more mindful of what's unfolding in your life and your children's lives. Mindful parenting is about moment-to-moment, open hearted and nonjudgmental attention. It's about seeing our children as they are, not as we want them to be. We let everything that unfolds in life be the curriculum for our parenting—because it is—whether we like it or not.

If this style of parenting appeals to you, then taking ten minutes to develop a mindful parenting plan will not only serve your children's well-being, but it will also make your relationship with your child more conscious, connected, and intentional.

Action Plan: Creating a mindful parenting plan involves deciding who you want to be as a parent, how you want to interact with your children, and what to do when those challenging, stressful situations come up.

The best way to begin is by assessing how you parent now and what you want to change in order to have a more mindful parenting style. You can do this by asking yourself a few questions:

- » Is my approach to parenting more responsive or reactive?
- » Do I tend to rush my children through life because of our busy schedules?
- » Am I distracted more often than not when I'm with my child?
- » Do I have a "my way or the highway" approach to rules, or do I listen to my child's opinions?
- » Do I frequently get angry, yell, and use corporal punishment?
- » When my children misbehave or act out, do I pause and then decide?
- » Do I just go through the motions of interacting with them?
- » Do I spend more time with digital devices than with my children?
- » When I spend time with my child, am I present and engaged?

As you answer these questions, make notes about areas where you could benefit from a more mindful approach. Even if you have been more reactive and distracted as a parent in the past, there is *still* plenty of time to change your patterns.

Here are seven ideas you can use to support your mindful parenting endeavors:

1. **Think about the person you want to be with your child.** When your child grows up and looks back on his or her childhood and you as a parent, who will they describe? What can you do to become more of the person you want your children to describe?

2. **Implement a "pause, reflect, respond" approach to conflict and bad behavior.** If your child yells or is disrespectful, you don't have to respond immediately. Step back, calm down, and think about how you want to respond and what you want to say.

3. **Consider slowing down your entire routine with your kids.** So much tension, stress, and frustration for both you and your child arise from rushing from one thing to the next. Allow more time between activities and think about cramming less into a day. Children need transition time and unstructured playtime.

4. **Establish an "electronics free" time during the day when your kids (and you) are completely disconnected from their phones, computers, game devices, and television.** These devices are not only distractions, but they also overstimulate children, making them more agitated and stressed.

5. **When you are with your children, be present.** Studies have shown that you don't have to spend a large quantity of time with your kids for them to turn out just fine. But the quality of the time you do spend with them is important. Whether it's a few hours or just fifteen minutes, make the time count by being present with them in whatever you are doing together.

6. **Listen to your children and pay attention to their words.** Let them know you are listening by looking them in the eye, reflecting back what you hear, and responding with love and care.

7. **Remember the brevity of childhood.** There are so many magical moments you can have with your children if you pay attention. The small, funny, carefree, happy little people they are now will disappear forever in a few short years. Prioritize

these magical moments over tasks and projects that aren't completely necessary. Remind yourself daily of what's truly important to you.

Learn More: For more information on mindful parenting, read the books *The Conscious Parent* by Dr. Shefali Tsabary and *Mindful Parenting: Simple and Powerful Solutions for Raising Creative, Engaged, Happy Kids in Today's Hectic World* by Kristen Race, PhD.

#65. Tame Your Longings and Cravings

One of the biggest challenges to living mindfully is dealing with our desire for "more." We long for more money, a happier relationship, a bigger home, a better job. We long for things to be the way they used to be or the way we planned for them to be. We long for an end to pain, disappointment, suffering, and unhappiness.

Our longings we feel in our gut are constantly simmering on low boil. We have a veil of discontent about our lives because we attach our happiness and peace of mind to having these longings met.

Our cravings are more visceral. They are the immediate itches that must be scratched. We crave our coffee in the morning to wake up and a cocktail in the evening to wind down. We crave a fix from our smartphones, the immediate gratification of checking email, and the narcotic effect of watching mindless television.

The more we give in to our longings and cravings, the more power they have over us. They keep us agitated, anxious, and frustrated. When our desires aren't fulfilled, when we can't have what we want, we loop our disappointments over and over in our minds, which intensifies our unhappy feelings.

There's nothing wrong with having goals or wanting to improve your circumstances. But when you become too attached to your longings and cravings, they get in the way of your ability to savor the present moment; then you are creating unnecessary suffering.

According to psychotherapist and author Sasha T. Loring, in an article for *Mindful*, "Much of our mental energy is focused on getting what we want. Fortunately the path of mindfulness is built around recognizing, loosening, and eventually liberating ourselves from this constant craving and grasping."

You may find that the end of the day is a time when your longings and attachments are the strongest. As you wind down, you have more time to fixate on what's missing from your life, how desperately you want it, and what you need to satisfy these cravings. The more you think about it, the more attached you become.

The truth is, when you become so attached to what you don't have, you have no availability for the beautiful reality in front of you. Says Byron Katie, author of the book *Loving What Is: Four Questions That Can Change Your Life*, "When we stop opposing reality, action becomes simple, fluid, kind, and fearless."

Taking ten minutes in the evening to examine your longings and cravings can set you on the path to releasing them. As you let go of your grip on "what isn't," you will discover a liberating sense of gratitude for what you do have in this moment. Life becomes easier and more peaceful.

Action Plan: Find a quiet space in your home where you won't be interrupted or distracted. Have a pen and paper handy to make notes.

Close your eyes and take several deep and cleansing breaths. Pay attention to your emotions and physical feelings. Notice any feelings of frustration, agitation, anxiety, disappointment, or anger. Notice any physical symptoms that might reflect these emotions—muscle pain, tightness, shortness of breath, or abdominal distress.

Silently ask yourself what you are longing for or craving that might be the cause of these negative emotions and physical sensations. What is your "wanting mind" fixated on? How do you feel unfulfilled? What thoughts are you attached to related to your longings? Write down whatever comes up for you as an answer.

Once you identify your longings and cravings, close your eyes again and review them as you observe your thoughts in meditation. Observe the longing as though it were a cloud floating through your consciousness. Recognize your longing as a thought that has no power over you.

Notice how your attention gets sidetracked and pulled away by your longings and cravings, and how you allow that to happen. Remind yourself that you are master of your attention, and choose to focus your attention on the present moment. Use your breathing as an anchor to help you with this focus during this exercise.

As your attention shifts to the present moment, see the present through a lens of gratitude and contentment. Allow the beauty and goodness of this moment to shine through so brightly that it blinds you to "what's missing." Even if the present moment isn't ideal, there is perfection in accepting and embracing what is.

Pay attention to any residual resistance to the present moment—any feelings of longing or dissatisfaction. Gently return your attention back to your breathing or your awareness of your surroundings.

When you finish this exercise, you will become more aware of longings and attachments in your daily life. Use that awareness to come back to center. Remind yourself that this moment is perfect, and you can release your longings to end your suffering.

Learn More: Check out Byron Katie's book *Loving What Is: Four Questions That Can Change Your Life* and *Letting Go: The Pathway of Surrender* by David R. Hawkins.

#66. Mindfully Review Your Day

Many people take time before a new year to review the previous year and what they've accomplished. They might look at the goals they set and how they fared at achieving them. This yearly review invites self-awareness and recalibration. It's an opportunity to acknowledge what you've done well and how you can improve moving forward.

An annual self-assessment is a valuable exercise when it comes to your major life goals. But leaving these reviews for the end of the year can prevent you from fully recognizing shifts and changes you could be making along the way to improve your quality of life.

As we've mentioned throughout this book, the most precious moment you will ever have is the one right now. The only reality you'll ever experience is this moment. So the best analysis you can perform on how you are doing in life is a check-in with how present and mindful you are on a daily basis.

You can't be fully present 100% of the time, but as you've learned through the exercises in this book, you can adjust your thoughts, behaviors, and life priorities to become more present.

If the idea of living mindfully is intriguing to you, then it's important to watch your progress, see what is working for you and what isn't, and challenge yourself to build your "mindfulness muscle" each and every day.

You've heard the saying, "What gets measured gets done," and that is true for the practice of mindfulness as much as any endeavor. Developing daily mindfulness habits takes patience, persistence, and commitment. But seeing your own progress and how these habits are impacting your state of mind will give you the motivation and desire to stick with it.

Says Toni Bernhard, J.D., in an article for *Psychology Today*, "The more we become aware of the ways in which our thoughts, emotions, speech, and actions haven't served us or others well, the more likely we'll be able to change our behavior in the future."

Action Plan: At the end of the day, when the house is quiet and you've finished all your tasks, sit down for a few minutes of self-reflection. Find a quiet place where you won't be interrupted or distracted.

Close your eyes and go through a short breathing exercise to calm and clear your mind.

First, think about any specific mindfulness habits or goals you have set for yourself in general or earlier in the day. Perhaps you wanted to journal in the morning or set intentions for your day. Maybe you determined to be more present with your family or coworkers. Or you had a plan to meditate during your lunch break.

Related to these specific mindfulness goals, how well did you do today? Did you remember to take action? Did you find the habits difficult, boring, or unhelpful? Or did these mindfulness actions improve your productivity, well-being, general contentment, and inner peace? What did you learn about yourself and the way your mind works?

If you experienced any challenges with your mindfulness efforts, what could you do differently, or how could you alter your actions to improve? How can you do better tomorrow?

After reflecting on the mindfulness goals or habits you established for yourself, go back and review your entire day. Look at the encounters you had with other people. Think back on how you felt physically and emotionally during the day. Consider how focused and productive you were in your work or daily activities.

In what interactions or situations were you unconscious and mindless? Were there times when you were reactive, unfocused, or distracted? Did you have periods when your mind was racing, looping, and longing?

Examine these situations carefully and pay attention to where you were, what you were doing, and what might have triggered them. Is there anything you could alter or change to become more mindful and present in circumstances like these going forward?

Were there any events or interactions during your day in which you responded mindfully, with thoughtfulness, focus, presence, and attention? Was this a natural reaction for you, or did you have to remind yourself to practice mindfulness? How did you feel during these situations? What could you use from them to help you in areas where you were more unconscious?

Of course, the goal here isn't to achieve perfection in your interactions and behaviors. That's an impossible goal and one that would interfere with the peace of mind that you're hoping to achieve.

The purpose is to grow in self-awareness so have more automatic mindful responses to the events of your life. In time, practicing mindfulness in all of your actions and interactions will be less of an exception and more of your norm.

Learn More: One way to build the mindful review habit is to keep a daily journal that you can use to track your progress down the road. While there are many types of journals, we recommend the Moleskine Passion Wellness Journal because it combines different aspects of personal development prompts with blank pages where you can include specific comments about your personal development journey.

#67. Plan for Tomorrow

An excellent follow-up habit after reviewing the day is to plan for tomorrow. Planning the next day on the night before not only saves you time in the morning, but it also gives you the opportunity to use what you just learned from the daily review.

You may be tempted to skip this habit because you want to relax in the evening, but taking just ten minutes to think about your goals and plans for tomorrow will give you a leg up on a potentially hectic morning.

The planning itself can be a mindfulness exercise, as can complete some of your morning readiness tasks the night before. Making your life calmer, simpler, and more streamlined supports all your mindfulness efforts, helping you focus on what's most important rather than *reacting* to whatever comes your way.

Much of your planning will be practical in nature, related to projects you need to complete, appointments to schedule, and obligations to fulfill. You can also complete tasks like making your lunch, getting your clothes prepared, and packing items that need to go with you in the car. If you have children, you can prepare their food and clothing as well.

You can also use this time to think about your mindfulness goals and what you want to improve on for tomorrow based on what you've learned in the previous days and weeks. If you don't plan for these efforts and mind shifts, you may forget to practice them. Mindfulness, like any habit, doesn't become natural until you practice it for several weeks.

Action Plan: Sit down with pen and paper, and take a few deep, cleansing breaths. Remove any distractions so you can focus completely on your planning.

Begin by reviewing any practical tasks that can make your morning run more smoothly, such as making lunches and preparing clothes. Write down a list of anything you can do tonight that you don't have to complete in the morning.

Next, list out any events, meetings, or appointments you have already scheduled for tomorrow, and write down how much time each of these activities will take and the time of day they will occur.

Think about your three main goals you want to accomplish for tomorrow, as discussed in habit #15. You may want to shift this from a morning habit to an evening habit to allow more time in the morning. Assign a generous amount of time to complete each of these tasks.

In addition to these three goals, are there any projects or tasks you left unfinished today (or earlier in the week) that you need to address tomorrow? If so, list them as well, assigning an amount of time you'll need to complete each one.

Be sure to factor in any mindfulness exercises you might want to include in your day, such as meditating, taking a music break, spending extra time with your family, etc., and include the amount of time you want to give to these habits during your day.

Roughly schedule out your day tomorrow, hour to hour, from morning until early evening, based on the goals and activities you listed. If you see you have crammed your schedule too full with little wiggle room, remove some of the lower-priority items. Give yourself plenty of time to complete your goals and tasks so you can mindfully focus on each activity without feeling distracted or pulled away.

Think about the ways you want to be more present and mindful during your day tomorrow: in your work, with the people around you, and with the simple activities of your day. List anything you want to focus on specifically tomorrow.

Close your eyes, and mentally review the day you have planned out for yourself tomorrow. See yourself going through all of the actions and tasks calmly and joyfully. Envision yourself being present for others and engaged in whatever you are doing.

Open your eyes, and put your planning list in a place where it will be handy in the morning. Begin taking action on any preparation tasks you intend to complete before bedtime.

Learn More: One of Steve's favorite books is *The Success Principles* by Jack Canfield. In it, you'll find sixty-four strategies for improving your life, including advice on how to plan out your day so you're focused on the tasks that truly matter.

#68. Practice a "Shut Down" Ritual

What are your typical habits during the hour before going to bed? Maybe you watch TV, spend time on social media, and check the news before turning out the light. Maybe your routine involves doing chores, getting the kids settled, or having a serious conversation with your spouse right before bed.

When Barrie's children were in school, she was shuttling them back and forth from extracurricular activities, sometimes arriving home as late as ten o'clock at night. After getting them settled and doing last-minute chores, she would crash in bed exhausted, with little transition between the hectic activities of the day and the time her head hit the pillow.

In spite of how busy your life might be or how tempted you are to stay connected to electronics, you can improve your physical (and mental) well-being simply by being more mindful of how you spend that time right before bed.

Television and electronics are stimulating and disruptive to sleep. What you watch or read can keep your brain on high alert, especially if the information is disturbing or agitating. The blue light emitted by screens on your digital devices and televisions hinders the production of melatonin, the hormone that controls your circadian rhythm, making it harder to fall asleep and stay asleep.

Having arguments or serious conversations before bed can stimulate adrenaline production and kick-start a cycle of rumination that prevents you from relaxing and falling asleep. Even doing physical tasks right up to bedtime can raise your heart rate and body temperature, making it hard to wind down and fall asleep.

Sleep is so critical to your mental and physical health and your overall quality of life. It impacts your ability to function optimally during the day, improving your concentration and productivity. Poor sleep is associated with all kinds of physical problems, including a greater risk of obesity, heart disease, and stroke. It's also linked to a higher risk of depression.

The takeaway here is that being careless about your sleep habits can be extremely detrimental to your health and happiness. Your actions in the hour before bedtime can make or break your ability to fall asleep quickly and impact the quality of your sleep. That's why we suggest a mindfulness habit of creating a soothing, sleep-inducing ritual before pulling up the covers and turning out the light.

Optimally, you would begin this ritual thirty minutes to an hour before bed. But you can begin by backing up your evening schedule by ten or fifteen minutes to set up a transition time that is relaxing. You can continue to add time to this habit by cutting out some of your evening activities that hinder your sleep.

Action Plan: There are a variety of actions you can take before bed that can help you relax, unwind, and prepare for a good night's sleep. You may not want to include all the actions we outline below, but you can choose those that feel the most calming to you and that can be reasonably incorporated into your schedule.

1. **Turn out the light earlier.** According to studies conducted by The National Sleep Foundation, most adults require seven to nine hours of sleep a night. But according to the CDC, a third of adults aren't getting enough sleep on a regular basis. Allowing for fifteen minutes to fall asleep, consider the time you need to turn out the light to get at least seven hours of sleep. If you have to wake up at 6:00 a.m., then you need to be asleep by 11:00 p.m. That means lights out at 10:45 or so. Start by backing up your lights-out time by ten minutes at first, working up to the optimal bedtime for your schedule.

2. **Set up your room for sleep.** The best environment for sleep is a quiet, dark, cool room. Cover your windows or wear a sleep mask to block light. Set your thermostat between 65 and 70 degrees, adjusting your blankets accordingly. If noise is a problem, consider using a white noise machine. Also declutter your sleep space, as it has the effect of decluttering your mind before bed.

3. **Turn off your electronics.** Don't undo the calm sleep environment you've created by turning on your television or computer. Shut down your devices, including your smartphone, before

bed to maintain this relaxed state of mind.

4. **Take a bath.** Dim the lights in your bathroom or use candles to create a quiet, soothing atmosphere. Fill your tub with warm water and add a sleep-inducing bath oil, like lavender oil, to your tub. The warm water can help soothe aching muscles and joints and relax your body before bed. Give yourself a few minutes after your bath to allow your body to cool down before getting in bed.

5. **Ask for a light touch massage.** If you have a partner willing to do this for you, ask for a light touch massage of your head, shoulders, and back. You don't want a deep tissue massage that might leave you sore, but rather one that is soothing and relaxing.

6. **Do some light, positive reading.** A few minutes of reading before bed can help you fall asleep, as long as what you are reading isn't upsetting or disruptive. The evening is a good time to read something uplifting and inspirational, as it fills your mind with thoughts that you take with you into sleep.

7. **Practice evening gratitude.** See habit #69 below for more details on gratitude journaling before bed. Or you can simply think about everything you are grateful for as you fall asleep. Rather than counting sheep, you can count your blessings, focusing on the joy you receive from each item on your list.

8. **Listen to Soothing Music.** Rather than having a sitcom or the news blaring in the background, turn on some soothing music as you wind down and get ready for bed. You might choose spa music, classical, or light jazz, or anything that you find relaxing. You can have this music playing as you get yourself ready for bed, take a bath, or read. If it helps you fall asleep, put in some

earphones and listen in bed.

9. **Meditate.** Practicing a short period of meditation before bed can help you detach from your thoughts and worries. It can also help you lower your heart rate and calm your breathing, putting your body in the best state for sleep.

10. **Do a progressive full-body relaxation exercise.** Before falling asleep while lying in bed, invite every part of your body to relax and release. Beginning with your toes and moving all the way up to your head, focus on each part of your body and mentally ask that part to relax. Breathe into each body part, feeling it get heavier and heavier. You may find you fall asleep during this exercise before you make it to your head.

11. **Say your prayers.** If you are a spiritual person, right before bed is a great time to get in touch with your higher self and the higher power you believe in. You can use this time to give up the day and your worries to a higher being so you can go to sleep with a peaceful mind.

Learn More: You can learn more evening habits and rituals to improve your health and well-being in the book *Daily Routine Makeover: Evening Edition: Evening Tactics to Preserve Your Health, Sleep Restfully and Power Up for Tomorrow* by Zoe McKey.

#69. Evening Gratitude Journaling

In the second mindfulness habit, we talked about how writing in a gratitude journal in the morning can dispel thoughts of dread and anxiety for the oncoming day and replace them with a positive attitude. The same rule applies in the evening, but in reverse.

By the time you're ready for bed, it has been a long day. Even if you've been consciously mindful over the past sixteen hours, you probably have accumulated some stress or even have experienced a few unresolved issues.

If you go to bed without achieving clarity of mind, the unresolved issues will keep the gears in your mind churning all night long, which will make it challenging to get a restful night's sleep.

On the other hand, if you keep a gratitude journal that you write in before bedtime, you can do wonders for improving your sleep. For instance, one study found this habit decreased depression, and another one discovered that showing evening gratitude increased optimism, sleep quality, and overall health and lowered blood pressure.

So if you want to have an easier night's sleep, with better sleep quality, please consider an evening gratitude journaling session.

Action Plan: This habit should be one of your final actions before putting your head on the pillow. That way, you'll go to sleep with *only* good thoughts in your head.

The process here is simple. First, make sure this journal is always next to your bed—even if you used it in the morning. That way, it will act as a visual cue to write down your thoughts.

Next, open it up and take a few minutes to reflect on your day. Think about the good things that happened and then take time to consider some of the challenges you experienced. Odds are, you'll realize that most of the "problems" you experienced are meaningless in the grand scheme of things.

Finally, write down your thoughts and what you're grateful for. Here are five examples of what you can jot down:

1. Write down a gratitude item in your journal using words like, like "I am grateful that I am healthy and well."

2. Pay attention to the rhythm of your heartbeat, and notice how warm and comfortable it is.

3. Direct your thoughts to other specifics of your body. Your muscles are sore—but sore in a good way, from exercise. Pay attention to your breathing: steady and even. Feel the soft sheets, the fluffy pillow, and the mattress that supports your body.

4. Think about what life would be like if you were physically worse off than you are. What if you had constant pain? What if you were paralyzed? Even if your body has problems, it could always be worse. Try to think of the negatives and how relatively lucky you are.

5. Try this type of positive thinking on two to three items or even people and then rest for the night.

Nighttime gratitude journaling doesn't need to be a time-consuming habit. In fact, you could do the gratitude exercises in your head as you lay your head on the pillow, instead of feeling like you have to write down why you're grateful.

Learn more: If you'd like to learn more about how to express gratitude, we recommend this simple prayer of gratitude.

#70. Use Aromatherapy

Aromatherapy is a form of alternative medicine that uses the essential oils from plants to affect both your physical and mental well-being. It works in two different ways—one is controversial and the other is based on established facts. Let's look at the controversial method first.

Aromatherapists claim that many oils have a direct effect on the body. Some oils are absorbed through the skin, entering our bloodstream. Other oils are absorbed through the mucus membrane, getting a direct path to the brain. According to the theory, once absorbed, the chemical properties of the concentrated oils will have the same (or greater) effect as consumption of the plant would have.

As an example, let's talk about the use of the ginger essential oil. Ginger is a well-known "healthy" plant. It reduces inflammation, reduces sugar cravings, supports digestion, and helps nutrients absorb into the body. All of this makes ginger a good plant to assist in healthy weight loss. Due to this fact, many aromatherapy "weight loss" mixtures will include ginger. And this is where the controversy comes in.

Holistic practitioners and aromatherapists will point to many studies that show the efficacy of these essential oils on a variety of ailments, while some scientists will say that such studies have not always been conducted the "right" way, and that the link between cause and causation is thin.

Who is right?

We can't say with 100% certainty. But while we don't believe every single claim about essential oils, we do believe there's a small physical and mental benefit from using these types of products.

This leads to the second way to use essential oils—activating your power of scent.

Our sense of smell is one of our most powerful senses.

Scent can evoke vivid and realistic memories. When we smell good things, we feel better. And when we smell bad things, these sensations conjure up negative emotions (and often give us painful reminders of the past).

Scent is a powerhouse, and aromatherapy is based on surrounding yourself with pleasant fragrances.

Finding a scent you enjoy will increase your overall happiness. It will reduce your stress, calm you down, and create a relaxing atmosphere.

Now, if you want to build an aromatherapy mindfulness habit, the simplest way to do it is in the evening, right before going to bed.

Action plan: There are four different ways to practice aromatherapy:

1. Water immersion. Mix oils with a carrier, add it to a bath, and then submerge your body. Many bath oils are based on this idea.
2. Topical application. Masseuses often use essential oils diluted with "carrier" base like jojoba oil. This can also be facial creams, body oils, lotions, and homemade essential oil blends.
3. Direct inhalation. This is simply opening a bottle of essential oil and taking a deep breath (while thinking happy thoughts).
4. Indirect inhalation. This is where diffusers come into play.

Diffusers are machines where you can add drops of the oil with a larger volume of water. The water is slowly vaporized, either by heat or ultrasonically. The resultant mist is mostly water mixed with trace amounts of the aromatic oils. This mist has a nice smell with some great potential health and mental benefits.

While all four methods work, we recommend using a diffuser because it's easy to use and incorporate into your daily routine. The specific essential oils we like are lavender, chamomile, bergamot, and ylang ylang because they are all great aids for getting a full night's rest.

Learn more: Aromatherapy is a pretty big topic. There are quite a few books and blogs dedicated to aromatherapy and the different methods of mixing essential oils. There are many premade blends available for purchase in addition to all the single essential oils. Then there are almost as many DIY blends as there are ways to cook shrimp.

If you want to find out more about the world of essential oils, Steve has a series of large posts on the topic. The best place to get started is his post about using essential oils for a good night's sleep. And he also has a review of five of the best essential oils diffusers.

#71. Practice Guided Sleep Meditation

We have already discussed the mindfulness benefits of meditation, but traditional meditation does require mental effort on your part—especially when you are just beginning. Regular meditation should be entered and practiced with a state of alert awareness, even as you become more calm and relaxed.

Guided meditation, however, is an excellent mindfulness habit to help you relax and go to sleep. With guided meditation, you are eased into a meditative state by a person who has recorded a meditation sequence. This guide will walk you through the process step by step, so that you don't have to do any of the mental work (except following instructions). You can simply listen, let go, and relax into sleep.

A guided sleep meditation often includes breathing exercises, a full-body relaxation sequence, imagery, and visualization, as well as soothing background music. In the best guided meditations, the guide will have a calm and soothing voice that doesn't distract you from relaxing into a restful state.

As you listen to the guide and follow the relaxation and sleep-inducing instructions, you will be less focused on your own thoughts and worries—thoughts that can keep you from falling asleep. The soothing effects of guided sleep meditations often result in you falling asleep before the meditation is over.

This is an excellent mindfulness habit to incorporate into your bedtime routine if you are someone who has trouble winding down and falling asleep. You can also use these guided meditations in the middle of the night if you awaken and can't go back to sleep.

Action Plan: Get a comfortable pair of earphones that you don't mind wearing when you fall asleep. Wearing earphones not only prevents you from disturbing your bedmate, but it also allows you to receive the meditation in a more direct and intimate way.

Research and listen to a few guided sleep meditations before you begin, as you want to ensure the guide and the content work well for you. Barrie particularly likes the guided sleep meditation called "Yoga Nidra for Sleep" with Jennifer Piercy and "Into Sleep" by Quiet Mind Cafe. You can find a variety of sleep meditations on YouTube, as well as dozens of apps with sleep meditations.

If you don't find a voice you like in one of these recorded guided meditations, you can always record yourself as the meditative guide. Your own voice is especially effective for inducing the relaxation response, as most of us tend to respond best to suggestions we provide ourselves. You can use this script as a guide for recording your own meditation, or you can write your own script that suits you.

Download or upload your chosen guided meditation onto your smartphone, iPad, or other device. Once you are in bed and ready to sleep, put in the earphones and turn on the guided meditation.

Learn More: If you find guided meditation enjoyable, you might enjoy this extensive library of guided meditations hosted by Tara Brach, founder of the Insight Meditation Community of Washington, DC.

PART VII

CONCLUSION

How to Build Your First Mindfulness Habit Routine

As you've seen, this book explores seventy-one mindfulness habits you can add to a daily schedule. That said, it's impossible to do all of them. Since each takes five to ten minutes to complete, it would take you six to twelve hours to do these habits. Trying to do so might make you a mindfulness habit expert, but you may neglect some of the real-world necessities that help you maintain your career, relationships, and lifestyle. (And you can certainly *apply mindfulness* to any of your life experiences and daily routines.)

We recommend starting small by building a single routine at a specific time each day that has a maximum of three habits covered in this book.

Do this for at least a month, and then once these habits become second nature, you can move on to building more habits *or* adding a new routine to a different time of the day.

To help you put this into action, we want to reinforce the importance of developing your habit creation skills. We recommend a thirteen-step strategy for building routines (that Steve discusses in his book *Habit Stacking*).

1. Identify an area of your life you want to improve. *Do you want to feel more energized in the mornings? Feel less stressed at*

work? Be "more present" at home with your family in the evening? Determine the biggest "pain" in your life, then build a mindfulness routine that will help you overcome it.

2. Pick mindfulness habits that don't require much willpower. For example: awaken with gratitude, make your bed mindfully, clean your desk, take a digital break, and practice walking meditation. Complete these activities for a few weeks until the routine is automatic, then add more habits.

Remember: even though there are seventy-one habits mentioned in this book, you only need to pick a few to create a positive change in your life.

3. Pick a time, location, or combination of both for when you'll complete this routine. We've included four times of day when you can practice mindfulness. Just think of the area of your life that you'd like to improve and build a routine around that time of day.

4. Anchor your stack to a trigger, which is an existing habit that you automatically do *every* day, like showering, brushing your teeth, checking your phone, going to the refrigerator, or sitting down at your desk. This is important because you need to be 100% certain that you won't miss this trigger.

5. Create a logical checklist, which should include the sequence of the habits, how long it takes to complete each item, and where you'll do them.

6. Be accountable by using an app like Coach.me to track your progress and frequently talking to an accountability partner with whom you share your breakthroughs, challenges, and future plans.

7. Create small enjoyable rewards that help you stick with this routine and hit important milestones. These rewards can include watching your favorite TV show, eating a healthy snack, or relaxing for a few minutes.

8. Focus on repetition by never missing a day. In fact, it's crucial that you stick to the routine—even if you need to skip one or two habits. Consistency is more important than anything else.

9. Avoid breaking the chain by eliminating any excuse for missing a day. Create a doable daily goal that can be achieved no matter what happens, and don't let yourself be talked out of it. Perhaps you'll set a small goal requiring you to only complete two or three actions. The important thing is to set a goal that can be achieved even when you have an off day.

10. Expect the occasional challenge or setback. In fact, it's better if you assume they will happen and then make a plan for how you'll handle them. If you get stuck, review the six challenges that we just covered and implement the advice for your unique obstacle.

11. Schedule the frequency of a stack by committing to this routine as a daily, weekly, or monthly series of actions. My suggestion is to get started with a simple daily routine, but when you want to build more habits, add a weekly or monthly task.

12. Scale up by adding more habits and increasing the total time of the routine. But be very cautious with this step. If you notice that it's getting progressively harder to get started (e.g., you're procrastinating), then either reduce the number of habits or ask yourself *why* you want to skip a day. The more you understand about your lack of motivation, the easier it will be to overcome it.

13. Build one routine at a time because each additional new routine increases the difficultly of sticking with your current habits. Only when *you* feel that a stack has become a permanent behavior should you consider adding a new routine.

That's it—thirteen steps to build a mindfulness routine that will create a positive, long-term change in your life. (If you'd like a printable version of these steps, **check out the PDF version that we've included on the companion site**.)

We won't lie and say it'll be easy 100% of the time, but if you stick to these steps, you can overcome any challenge that comes your way. By the way, even if you have a setback with these steps, if you work on them mindfully, you'll still reinforce your new mindfulness practice!

Final Thoughts on Mindfulness Habits

Although we've outlined many mindfulness habits in this book, *the practice* of mindfulness is so much more than adopting a set of positive new behaviors. It's more than a novel self-help technique or a drug-free way to deal with stress.

Mindfulness is a way of life.

It's a *choice* for embracing every moment as though it's your last.

Mindfulness is also a process of letting go. You let go of your worry about the future and your regrets about the past. You let go of negative, painful thoughts that cause you suffering. You let go of attachments to people and things that distract and agitate you. You let go of the need to control life but instead allow it to flow naturally and joyfully— moment by moment.

Most of us live under the illusion that all of our cares, worries, hopes, dreams, and longings are urgently important and vividly real. But they are not. They are the ethereal dust clouds of our own anxious imaginings. What IS real is *now*. Right now. This perfect moment. Will you wake up to it? Will you choose to live in it?

Thích Nhất Hạnh says, "Today, you can decide to walk in freedom. You can choose to walk differently. You can walk as a free person, enjoying every step."

We're not suggesting it's easy to take this walk. Living in the moment, every moment, is like balancing on the tip of a pin. But as you practice the habits of mindfulness, and as you embrace mindfulness as your way of life, you'll find your footing and become more adept at being present.

As a byproduct of your efforts, you will make vast improvements in reducing your anxiety, minimizing stress, and becoming mentally and physically healthier. You will improve your relationships, find more joy in your work, and discover pleasure in things you previously overlooked or avoided.

On occasion, you may hear a little voice in the back of your mind telling you that there are better, more urgent things to do with your time. When you find yourself in this position, go to a quiet place, close the door, acknowledge your emotions, breathe, and remind yourself to "be here now." There is no better place to be.

We've given you seventy-one ideas for practicing mindfulness. These are tools that you can incorporate into your day to help you remain present, even as the world pulls you into its distractions, obligations, and amusements. We all need tools to help us initiate change and stay committed to our efforts, and that's what we hope we've provided with this book.

But if you practice no other habit from this book but one, please make it this: just pay attention. Pay attention to what you are doing right now for as many "right nows" as you can remember. If you do that, you have embraced mindfulness.

We wish you the best of luck and encourage you to *be present*—starting now!

Cheers,

Barrie Davenport & Steve Scott

One Last Reminder ...

We've covered a wealth of information in this book, but that doesn't mean your self-educational efforts should end here. In fact, we've created a small companion website that includes many resources mentioned throughout *10-Minute Mindfulness*.

Here are just a few things we've included:

» The 13-step quick start checklist to quickly identify the best mindfulness habits and then build a routine around these actions.

» Each link and resource mentioned in this book.

» The gratitude worksheet in a downloadable PDF file.

» An extensive list of positive affirmations in a downloadable PDF file.

» Mindfulness questions for couples in a downloadable PDF file.

» A video walkthrough of the Headspace App

» A list of 155 ways to reward yourself for accomplishing a goal or task.

Plus, we will be adding more goodies to this website in the months to come. So, if you're interested in expanding on what you've learned in this book, then click this link and join us today:

http://mindfulnesshabit.com/10mm

Thank You!

Before you go, we'd like to say thank you for purchasing our book.

You could have picked from dozens of books on habit development, but you took a chance and checked out this one.

So, big thanks for downloading this book and reading all the way to the end.

Now we'd like ask for a small favor. **Could you please take a minute or two and leave a review for this book on Amazon?**

This feedback will help us continue to write the kind of Kindle books that help you get results. And if you loved it, please let us know. 😊

More Books by Steve

» Novice to Expert: 6 Steps to Learn Anything, Increase Your Knowledge, and Master New Skills

» Declutter Your Mind: How to Stop Worrying, Relieve Anxiety, and Eliminate Negative Thinking

» The Miracle Morning for Writers: How to Build a Writing Ritual That Increases Your Impact and Your Income

» 10-Minute Digital Declutter: The Simple Habit to Eliminate Technology Overload

» 10-Minute Declutter: The Stress-Free Habit for Simplifying Your Home

» The Accountability Manifesto: How Accountability Helps You Stick to Goals

» Confident You: An Introvert's Guide to Success in Life and Business

» Exercise Every Day: 32 Tactics for Building the Exercise Habit (Even If You Hate Working Out)

» The Daily Entrepreneur: 33 Success Habits for Small Business Owners, Freelancers and Aspiring 9-to-5 Escape Artists

» Master Evernote: The Unofficial Guide to Organizing Your Life with Evernote (Plus 75 Ideas for Getting Started)

» Bad Habits No More: 25 Steps to Break Any Bad Habit

» Habit Stacking: 97 Small Life Changes That Take Five Minutes or Less

» To-Do List Makeover: A Simple Guide to Getting the Important Things Done

» 23 Anti-Procrastination Habits: Overcome Your Procrastination and Get Results in Your Life

» S.M.A.R.T. Goals Made Simple: 10 Steps to Master Your Personal and Career Goals

» 115 Productivity Apps to Maximize Your Time: Apps for iPhone, iPad, Android, Kindle Fire and PC/iOS Desktop Computers

» Writing Habit Mastery: How to Write 2,000 Words a Day and Forever Cure Writer's Block

» Daily Inbox Zero: 9 Proven Steps to Eliminate Email Overload

» Wake Up Successful: How to Increase Your Energy and Achieve Any Goal with a Morning Routine

» 10,000 Steps Blueprint: The Daily Walking Habit for Healthy Weight Loss and Lifelong Fitness

» 70 Healthy Habits: How to Eat Better, Feel Great, Get More Energy and Live a Healthy Lifestyle

» Resolutions That Stick! How 12 Habits Can Transform Your New Year

More Books by Barrie

» Declutter Your Mind: How to Stop Worrying, Relieve Anxiety, and Eliminate Negative Thinking

» 10-Minute Digital Declutter: The Simple Habit to Eliminate Technology Overload

» 10-Minute Declutter: The Stress-Free Habit for Simplifying Your Home

» 201 Relationship Questions: The Couple's Guide to Building Trust and Emotional Intimacy

» Self-Discovery Questions: 155 Breakthrough Questions to Accelerate Massive Action

» Sticky Habits: 6 Simple Steps to Create Good Habits That Stick

» Finely Tuned: How To Thrive As A Highly Sensitive Person or Empath

» Peace of Mindfulness: Everyday Rituals to Conquer Anxiety and Claim Unlimited Inner Peace

» Confidence Hacks: 99 Small Actions to Massively Boost Your Confidence

» Building Confidence: Get Motivated, Overcome Social Fear, Be Assertive, and Empower Your Life for Success

» The 52-Week Life Passion Project: The Path to Uncover Your Life Passion

Made in the USA
San Bernardino, CA
20 October 2017